FORT JESUP

FORT JESUP

A HISTORY

SCOTT DeBOSE

THE
History
PRESS

Published by The History Press
Charleston, SC
www.historypress.com

Front cover, bottom: Reconstructed officer's quarters at Fort Jesup State Historic Site. *Photo by author.*
Back cover, top: Original kitchen at Fort Jesup State Historic Site. *Photo by author.*
Center: Zachary Taylor. *Library of Congress.*

First published 2022

Manufactured in the United States

ISBN 9781467153256

Library of Congress Control Number: 2022943530

CONTENTS

ACKNOWLEDGEMENTS

I would like to thank my family, who has endured my obsession with history and Fort Jesup for many years—especially my wife, Courtney, who not only puts up with shelves of books and boxes of papers but helped with countless hours of proofreading and editing of this work, taking the ramblings of a historian and helping turn them into a work that is more accessible, understandable and enjoyable.

INTRODUCTION

Fort Jesup was established to fight a war. Not in an aggressive sense, not in a saber-rattling or politically threatening way; it was founded out of the realization that, one day, the United States and whoever controlled the area known as Texas would become involved in an armed conflict. In fact, even before Fort Jesup was founded, there were four conflicts between Americans and the Spanish in Texas, one of which almost erupted into a full-scale war with Spain.

The fort was founded a day's march from the international boundary in what had been a disputed area less than a year before, and the soldiers were called on to help open the region for settlement through exploration, building roads, clearing rivers, protecting travelers from outlaws, negotiating with Native tribes and representing the United States in international affairs, all while building their fort by hand, growing much of their own food and practicing the military arts on the parade ground. Thousands of travelers on their way to Texas would pass by the fort, often stopping to rest and resupply. Many of these travelers' names have been lost in the mass of humanity, but some, such as William Travis, were destined to shape American history. More than just a fort in the wilderness, Fort Jesup was home to hundreds of soldiers, officers, women, children and civilians, all with different backgrounds, ethnicities and social classes, who were trying to survive and thrive in a military environment on the edge of civilization.

Fort Jesup as a military post was never attacked, but soldiers from the fort would be called on to fight and die in five wars: the Texas Revolution, the Second Seminole War, the Mexican-American War, the Civil War and World War II. Lessons learned on the parade ground would serve both soldiers and officers well in these conflicts, and many of the young officers of the post would rise through the ranks to command armies on both sides of the Civil War. Many names familiar to students of military history spent time at Fort Jesup: Zachary Taylor, Ulysses S. Grant, James Longstreet, William Hardee, Don Buell, Edmund P. Gaines, William S. Harney, Ethan Hitchcock, Stephen Kearny, Henry Leavenworth, Winfield Scott, surgeons general Thomas Lawson and Joseph K. Barnes (who treated Abraham Lincoln after he was shot at Ford's Theater) and dozens more officers who would become generals in the Mexican-American War and the Civil War. The fort was also home to Dred Scott, of the famous Supreme Court case. The twentieth century would see another future general using Fort Jesup as a training ground, George S. Patton.

With so many famous officers connected to the post and so much national attention focused there in the nineteenth century, one would assume that Fort Jesup's place in American history would be secured. However, that is not the case. Even though Fort Jesup is listed on the National Register of Historic Places, has been declared a National Historical Landmark by Congress, is a State Historic Site managed by the State of Louisiana, is part of the Cane River National Heritage Area and is located along El Camino Real de los Tejas National Historic trial, the post's role in American history has been largely forgotten. This is due in large part to a couple of historical ironies. First, the fort is attached to the "wrong" war. American history is often thought of as only having a handful of events: the pilgrims land; no taxation without representation leads to the American Revolution; then, a short time later, the Civil War breaks out. People may "remember the Alamo," but they know little of the history of the conflict or its broader connections to U.S. history—outside of the Disney movie and maybe when John Wayne played Davy Crockett. The Mexican-American War has been largely overshadowed by the Civil War, in part because the scale of the Civil War was so massive (every American was touched in some way by the Civil War, as compared to the Mexican-American War, in which only a few thousand soldiers were in the field at any one time).

The other irony is how time has treated the site itself. The community of Fort Jesup thrived until the early twentieth century, and it was always a farming community with a decent-sized population—but not as large as many other towns in Louisiana. The old fort was used as a high school/college and later became one of the first public high schools in Sabine

Parish, but when a fire destroyed many of the old buildings, the school was moved to the parish seat, and when the railroad missed the town by a few miles, it started a steady decline in the population of the community. By the time efforts were started to save the old fort, all that was left was one of the enlisted men's kitchens/mess halls built circa 1837 and a few stone foundations, the only remains of the once-proud military reservation that at its height had over one hundred buildings and a garrison of over one thousand officers and men (at a time when there were only slightly more than six thousand soldiers on active duty in the entire U.S. Army), with land extending three miles in each direction from the flagstaff. Today, the site is a lovely park setting with a picnic area, ponds, 20 acres of land (out of the original 16,902 acres), one historic building and one reconstructed officer's quarters, which is used as a museum and visitor center. But this appearance is misleading and reinforces the idea that Fort Jesup was not important; in fact, most visitors to the historic site have the first impression that the site was a plantation home, due to the fact that the architecture of the officer's quarters and the historic kitchen can barely be seen from the parking lot. There were never walls around Fort Jesup, which adds to the confusion of "Where's the fort?" (yes, staff of the historic site are really asked that question).

Like many children in Sabine Parish, my first memories of visiting Fort Jesup were not historical reenactments or living history events but going to family reunions and civic club meetings that my parents dragged me to. Being fascinated with the Civil War at a young age, I loved being at a "fort" but had no idea of its history, and I fell into the same trap as many people, believing that Fort Jesup was just a small outpost set up to chase outlaws out of "no man's land" by a guy who would later be president (though I had never heard of him), that the fort was not a Civil War site but was built earlier and had vague connections to the Mexican-American War, which I had never heard of until I saw the exhibit about it at the site, and that the post had only a few buildings, a few soldiers and was neat but just not that important. Later field trips to the site would shed a little light, but it would not be until I started volunteering at the historic site in the summer of 1995 and later joined the staff as a tour guide and, in college, became a lab assistant during one of the archaeology field schools held at the site that I began to see what Fort Jesup really was and why it was so important. Even at that time, it was still hard to make connections between the fort and important people and events in American history—we had few historical documents in the museum library and few books had been written—but each year, as I researched more and more and gathered more primary and secondary sources, the story of Fort Jesup became clearer.

This book has been a work in progress for over twenty years, starting in 1995 when as a tenth grader I spent my first day in the parish library going through records and being disappointed in just how few sources there were but excited by those I could find. Since that day, it has been my goal to write a book about this important historical fort, and I have spent the last two decades gathering sources and trying to connect the historical "dots." It is my hope that this work will show Americans everywhere how an "isolated" fort in the Louisiana wilderness played a key but often overlooked role in shaping American history and our lives today.

Opposite: Map of Fort Jesup circa 1846 from an early park brochure. *Courtesy of the Louisiana Office of State Parks, Fort Jesup State Historic Site.*

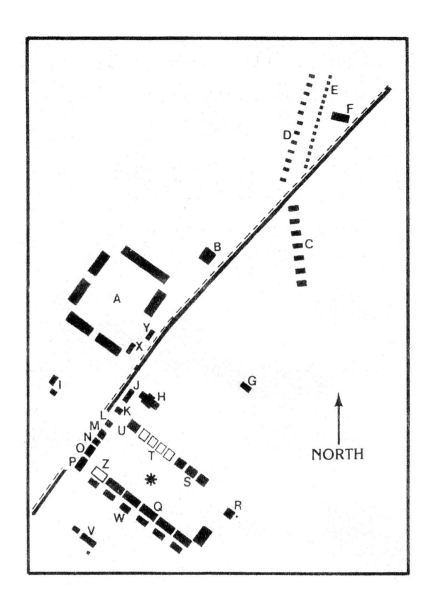

A. Dragoon Stables	**I.** Officers' Quarters No. 3	**S.** Officers' Quarters (New)
B. Stable	**J.** Storehouse	**T.** Officers' Quarters (Old)
C. Blissville	**K.** Powder Magazine	**U.** Adjutant's Office
D. Soldiers' Quarters, 3rd Infantry	**L.** Guardhouse	**V.** Hospital
E. Officers' Quarters, 3rd Infantry	**M.** Adjutant's Office, 3rd Infantry	**W.** Kitchens, Soldiers' Quarters
F. Mess House, 3rd Infantry	**N.** Quartermaster's Office	**X.** Band Quarters
	O. Quartermaster's Store	**Y.** Soldiers' Quarters
G. Officers' Quarters No. 1	**P.** Commissary Store	**Z.** Officers' Quarters
H. Officers' Quarters No. 2	**Q.** Soldiers' Quarters	
	R. Cottage	* Parade Ground

CHAPTER 1

THE WESTERN BOUNDARY OF THE UNITED STATES AND THE ORIGIN OF FORT JESUP

W hen the Louisiana Purchase of 1803 failed to define the western boundary of the territory, it created a diplomatic crisis between the United States and Spain. Not only was Spain concerned over the illegal immigration of Americans from Louisiana into Texas, but even more alarming were the United States government's claims that Texas was also part of the Louisiana Purchase. Spain maintained that the Arroyo Hondo (a small creek between Natchitoches and modern-day Robeline) had always been the border between Louisiana and Texas, even when Spain owned both, while the Jefferson administration claimed that the Rio Grande was the boundary of the Louisiana Purchase. By 1806, the border dispute was on the verge of open warfare as Spain began reenforcing its garrisons in Texas and Spanish troops crossed the Sabine River to establish outposts between the Sabine River and Natchitoches.

The American response was to send Major General James Wilkinson, the commanding general of the U.S. Army, along with additional infantry and artillery to reenforce Fort Claiborne with instructions to, if necessary, march to the Sabine. However, patriotism would not be the only factor motivating Wilkinson's decisions. Not only was he the commanding general of the U.S. Army, but Wilkinson was also a Spanish spy, known as Agent Thirteen, and he was involved with former vice president Aaron Burr's plot to conquer Mexico, Texas and large regions of the Ohio and Mississippi Valleys to create a new empire, with Burr as King and Wilkinson as military leader and second-in-command.

Wilkinson now found himself trying to please three masters, all with conflicting interests. Burr needed a war with Spain to justify his invasion of Mexico and to distract the small U.S. Army, while Burr made his move to separate the western territories, which felt isolated and abandoned by U.S. economic policies that favored the East Coast. The United States, while willing to go to war over the boundary, was ill prepared to challenge the Spanish global empire, which was still allied to Napoleon. War might have brought glory for Wilkinson, but there was an equal chance that war could bring disgrace and the loss of his prestige and position. There was also the fear in Wilkinson's mind that, in a time of war, Spain would expect Wilkinson to act in their best interests, considering the large sums of gold they had paid him over the last decade—or worse, Spain might reveal his secret identity, leading to his disgrace and possible execution for treason. Instead of picking a side, Wilkinson decided to play all sides against the middle to save his own hide. Wilkinson quickly negotiated an agreement with the Spanish commander to create a neutral ground or "No Man's Land" between the Sabine River and the Arroyo Hondo and then marched to New Orleans to arrest Burr before he could enter the city. Wilkinson even testified as the government's star witness at Burr's trail. Burr was found not guilty of treason due to lack of evidence. But in the court of public opinion, both Burr and Wilkinson were considered guilty by most Americans. Wilkinson retained his position in the army until 1813, when he was forced to resign after a series of defeats in the War of 1812. He moved to Mexico and died in Mexico City in 1825.

Wilkinson may have saved his position and prevented a war, but he left the United States with a roughly five thousand-square-mile strip of land that neither Spain nor the United States could station troops in, exercise control over or police. The so-called Neutral Strip soon became a haven for outlaws, who would commit crimes in the United States and Spain and then run to No Man's Land to avoid prosecution. Traders and merchants traveling along the road between Natchitoches and Nacogdoches became easy targets, and many an unwary traveler met a violent end in No Man's Land. Slave traders, smugglers and American adventurers who joined various illegal expeditions to help the Mexican win their independence from Spain all set up operations in the strip. Hundreds of other American settlers entered No Man's Land, willing to brave the danger of the lawless region for the free land, while an unknown number of Spanish refugees fleeing the Mexican Revolution made

This page: Park volunteers portraying early settlers. *Photos by author.*

new homes in the region, joining the Spanish subjects who had received land grants from Spain in the late eighteenth century.[1]

Starting in 1817, negotiations between Secretary of State John Quincy Adams and Spanish minister Luis de Onis began to determine where the western boundary would be. On February 22, 1819, a treaty was signed. Titled the Transcontinental Agreement (and referred to as the Adams Onis Treaty), the document transferred all of Florida to the United States and set the boundary between Spanish territory and the United States at the Sabine River; in exchange, Spain received undisputed possession of Texas. Ratification of the treaty would be delayed for two years, until 1821, by both the U.S. Senate and King Ferdinand VII of Spain as the legal status of recent land grants was determined. On February 22, 1821, exactly two years after it had been signed, King Ferdinand VII approved the Transcontinental Agreement. But the agreement only lasted for two days, because on February 24, the king signed a proclamation providing for the independence of Mexico and all the provinces, including Texas. The United States quickly recognized Mexico as an independent country and reaffirmed the boundary at the Sabine River.[2]

With the independence of Mexico in 1821, the era of No Man's Land officially came to an end. Seven Louisiana parishes would eventually be created out of the region: Allen, Beauregard, Desoto, Calcasieu, part of Natchitoches, Sabine and Vernon. While the Neutral Strip would soon be open to settlement and would see a wave of travelers heading to Texas, it would be decades before law and order would be brought to the region. Louisiana governor Pierre Villere pressed the War Department for a permanent military post near the Sabine River to protect the western boundary and help civilize the Neutral Strip. After the new international boundary was created and the First Seminole War along the Georgia/Florida border ended, the War Department began reassigning units, and the Seventh Infantry was selected to guard the western boundary of the United States.

The Seventh United States Infantry was originally organized on July 16, 1798, during the military buildup for a possible war with France, but with the negotiation of several treaties, the war scare diminished, and the unit was mustered out of service on June 15, 1800. As relations with Great Britain worsened during the first decade of the nineteenth century, Congress expanded the military and created several new regiments, including a reorganized Seventh Infantry, which was created on April 12, 1808. During the War of 1812, the regiment was involved in the battle of Fort Harrison on September 4 and 5, 1812, and the battle of New Orleans in December 1814 and January 1815. After the war, the Seventh fell victim to the Army Reduction Act, which not only reduced the size of the regiments but also eliminated dozens of regiments and randomly combined the remaining units. The Second, Third, Seventh, and Forty-Fourth regiments were all combined to create the new First Infantry and the Eighth, Nineteenth, Thirty-Sixth and Thirty-Eighth regiments were consolidated to form the new Seventh Infantry.[3]

The new Seventh was sent to the Florida/Georgia border, close to modern-day Tallahassee, to guard the southern border with Spanish Florida. When the Seventh arrived on the border at Fort Scott in 1816, the situation was tense. General Edmund P. Gaines, the American commander for the region, was adamant that white settlers would be safe on their lands, but he was equally forceful that the rights of the Indians would also be protected and that white settlers who settled illegally on tribal lands would not be protected. A series of cross-border raids by both sides increased hostilities. In 1817, open warfare broke out when a detachment of the Seventh was ambushed and massacred, starting the first of three Seminole Wars. The Seventh would fight in several battles of the war until peace was declared about a year later, and the unit remained in the region until 1821.[4]

Around the first of August 1821, the Seventh Infantry received news that they would be leaving Georgia for Louisiana and Arkansas and soon left Fort Scott, Georgia, and traveled down the Apalachicola River, arriving at the coast on October 4, where the troops camped for about six days while supplies were transferred to the transports that would carry the force to New Orleans. The weather turned wet, and rain fell for almost the entire six days that they were in camp. Finally, General Arbuckle's command was picked up by three or four ships for the ocean passage to New Orleans.[5]

Two accounts have survived of the journey from Fort Scott to what would eventually become Fort Jesup. One was written by Captain George Birch and the other by an enlisted soldier, Charles Martian Gray. Gray was born in 1800 in South Carolina and had dreamed of being a soldier since he was young. He tried to enlist during the War of 1812 but was too young. After the war, he ran away to enlist but was discovered by his father. Finally, at the age of nineteen, his father allowed him to enlist (enlistment age was twenty-one in the early 1800s without parental consent or proof that you were an orphan). Birch was born in England and immigrated to the United States before 1808. He joined the U.S. Light Dragoons in 1808 and fought in the War of 1812. After the reorganization of the army in 1815, he was transferred to the Seventh Infantry in 1815 as a captain.[6]

The Seventh Infantry embarked on October 10, 1821. George Birch wrote in his journal that the "breeze freshened from the SE we stood before it." The next morning,

> *my Ordly* [sic] *Sergeant reported one of the sick men dead* [sic], *I accordingly gave orders for the funeral which was conducted in the following manner, the corps was sewed up in a blankett* [sic] *with about fifteen or twenty pounds of iron attached to his feet then laid upon a plank, one end of which was put over the lee side of the vessel, the other was held by a soldier, and a soldier at service order on each side, while the music played the dead march the soldier at the head of the plank was then ordered to raise it up when a volley was fired and he launched feet foremost into the deep and seen no more.[7]*

The ships continued their passage west, anchoring for the night of October 12 at Ship Island, but on October 13, a storm blew in, and as Charles M. Grey recalled:

> *The troops had a stormy passage, were blown out into the Gulf stream, had the decks of their vessels swept by the turbulent surging waves.... The wives and children too of several of them were on board, and the hatches closed upon them. Their cries, and the wringing of hands, and prayers, and shrieks of despair, beggar description. The men were wrought upon nearly as much as the women, and the author well recollects that, amid the roaring of the waters, the swift-winged flashes of lighting that played the shrouds of his good ship, and the billows swelling mountain high, a stout-hearted friend of his, that nothing could daunt on land, in agony of his grief and desperation, yelled like a child, and prayed to God only for a little spot of land, upon which he said, in a state of frenzy, that if he could be spared to place his feet, he would paw up the ground like a young bull and perform such other various antics as were never before witnessed under high heaven. But through the mercy of God, all the vessels were permitted to reach their destination.[8]*

The ships arrived on October 13 at the Bay of St. Louis; on the fourteenth, the ships passed the Rigolets, they passed near the Lake Pontchartrain Lighthouse on the fifteenth, and on the sixteenth, the troops disembarked at Bayou St. John, where the command camped for a few days. The troops marched through New Orleans on October 26, 1821, and set up camp about half a mile above the city while waiting on transport ships to carry them up the Mississippi River. The transports arrived about two weeks later, on November 6. During the time at New Orleans, the men rapidly became sick and demoralized from scurvy, dysentery and the "dissipations of a city life…with all their vigor and virulence."[9]

It was during their stay at Bay St. Louis that the regiment's new lieutenant colonel, Zachary Taylor, joined the command. Taylor was born on November 24, 1784, in Orange County, Virginia, and was the third son of Richard Taylor, who had served as lieutenant colonel of the First Virginia Continentals during the American Revolution. His father had earned a large land bonus in Kentucky for his service in the Revolution, and he moved his family to the frontier when Zachary was two years old. Taylor joined the Regular Army in May 1808, receiving a commission as a first lieutenant in the Seventh U.S. Infantry. He was promoted to captain in 1810 and placed in command of Fort Knox until he was transferred a year later to command Fort Harrison. For his heroism in the defense of Fort Harrison when the post was attacked by Tecumseh and over four hundred Native warriors, Taylor was promoted to brevet major, but with the end of the war and the reduction in size of the army, Taylor—along with dozens of other officers—was asked to take a reduction in rank. Rather than taking a demotion to captain, Taylor chose to leave the army, but less than a year later, President Madison, a friend of the family, had him reinstated as a major. Taylor was promoted to lieutenant colonel in 1819; after the reduction of 1821, he maintained his rank but was transferred to the Seventh Infantry.[10]

The entire regiment traveled up the Mississippi River together until they reached the Red River. Once there, one part of the command was ordered to Arkansas under the command of Colonel Arbuckle and the other to the Red River under the command of Taylor. The whole command halted a few hours at the mouth of the Red River, then the Steamboat *Tennessee* with the Arkansas command proceeded up the Mississippi River and the steamboats *Arkansas* and *Couvior* entered the Red River. The Red River, named for the red color of its waters, appeared to Captain Birch to "be notorious for alligators," because even in the cold weather he "counted 62 on the sunny side of the bank within the space of 100 yards." One of the officers shot several of them from the deck of the boat.[11]

The *Couvior* (which Birch was on) arrived at Alexandria on November 14, 1821; however, the crew and troops on the *Arkansas* were not as fortunate.

Captain Birch recorded that "the other unfortunately burst her boiler and scalded five or six men two of which died the next morning, and after repairing, which took them about two weeks she arrived at this place." Although Captain Birch does not refer to it in his account, Gray accused the captain of the *Arkansas* of racing with another ship while intoxicated. To pull ahead of the other ship, Captain Black of the *Arkansas* opened the speed wheel of his ship to full, which caused the boiler to explode.[12]

Once the boats and passengers were reunited at Alexandria, the command began preparing to travel up the Red River. To travel up the Red River past the falls (or *rapides*, in French, from which Rapides Parish got its name), baggage and supplies were unloaded from the larger ships, carried overland above the falls and placed in keelboats (flat-bottomed, low-draft boats that had to be poled against the current). It took five weeks for the battalion to procure three keelboats large enough to transport the men over the rapids. The command departed Alexandria on December 5 and "proceeded up the river by cordelling [*sic*], as it's called in this part of the country." Crossing the rapids was hard, dangerous work. "The men, by most strenuous exertions, and by exposing themselves most freely to the water, in mid-winter, passed the first Rapids the first day, and encamped the second a mile distant, at night, where four of the men actually died in their sleep," as surgeon Lawson said, "from having taxed their strength and endurance too much in the water during the day." Gray wrote that "the names of these poor fellows were Burress, Jackson, Johnson 1st and Johnson 2nd, who were the next morning wrapped in their blankets, and all four laid together, without coffin or winding sheet, in a hole that had been dug out for the purpose, there 'to sleep their last sleep' 'unhonored and unsung' till the last trump shall assemble their dust to the great congregation that shall be gathered from the four corners of the earth, to hear the final doom of man."[13]

The troops arrived in Natchitoches on December 16, and on the seventeenth, they arrived at the site of Fort Selden, after traveling, as Captain Birch described, a distance of "thirteen hundred miles…under every disadvantage, in the height of the sickly season, and during the whole passage having bad weather our sick died off very fast, out of my company I lost ten on the passage (two of which died a day or two after our arrival)." Gray recorded that "they proceeded for about five days, during rain, and sleet and storm until they reached Natchitoches.…When they hove in sight of this little town, the troops made a sudden halt to bury two more of their number, Corporal Thompson and Samuel Pinson, who had paid the last debt of nature on the route, who were consigned to mother earth in the same primitive style as their comrades just mentioned above."[14]

In 1821, Natchitoches was described as a town "full of strangers and every place crowded and goods and wagons carrying things out to Sabine and Nacogdoches and droves of horses and mules packing for San Antonio."[15] As the troops entered Natchitoches on Sunday around three o'clock, an argument broke out between Zachary Taylor and David Twiggs. As was the military tradition, Twiggs ordered the musicians to play as the troops entered the town, but Taylor ordered the musicians to stop on the grounds that it was a Sunday. According to Gray, the argument became very heated, and "Twiggs cursed him [Taylor] and Taylor replied by reminding him in an imperative manner that he was his commanding officer."[16]

Taylor relieved the remaining companies of the First Infantry camped outside the town and ordered them to proceed to Baton Rouge. Taylor wanted to move his troops out of Natchitoches as soon as possible to prevent the temptations of saloons, billiard halls, gambling and prostitutes from dissolving the discipline of his command. Even if Taylor wanted to house his troops in town, there were not enough quarters or storehouses available. Fort Claiborne was in such a state of decay that it was next to useless as a shelter. Taylor, taking the advice of General Gaines, reoccupied the site of Fort Selden ten miles west of town. Even though the site had been abandoned for about two years, it was in better shape than Fort Claiborne and had the advantage of not being close to the distractions of Natchitoches. Taylor put his men to work repairing the post while awaiting the arrival of General Gaines, who would approve the location of the new fort closer to the Sabine. Gaines instructed Taylor to begin scouting the area west of Natchitoches for a suitable spot for the new post that would "combine the advantages of Defense and Health and afford protection to the Frontier inhabitants."[17]

For Taylor's weary soldiers, Fort Selden provided little comfort. Since the post had been abandoned for a couple of years, the command "found the fort in ruins and was obliged to pitch our tents finding only shelter enough for the sick and stores the weather being very cold." Gray described it as "an old rotten Fort." Taylor immediately put the men to work repairing the post and building new shelters, and as Gray recalled, "The troops went briskly to work repairing the Fort, knowing though they could not remain long at such a position, especially as the health of the men grew worse."[18]

During the repairs, it was Gray's turn to serve as cook, and one day, he saw a strange occurrence:

While diligently attending to my duties and such one day, and preparing a meal for my mess, I heard the dead march, and saw a funeral procession, or rather a burial detail passing along carrying to her grave, Mrs. Glenn, an old camp follower, or "Vivandiere" of the army, whose exuberant spirts, fun and frolic had enabled the soldiers to while away many a tedious hour. As the solemn cortege arrived opposite where I was cooking, the Assembly beat for the troops to draw their rations of whiskey and go to dinner. They deliberately laid the old woman down, and left her alone until they had drawn and drunk their liquor, and on their return, Paddy Flinn, a gibing Irishman, says to the others, "Boys we must bury the d—ed old b—h with her face down, to keep her from scratching out, for if she were in hell, she has so many pranks, and crooks, and turns, that the Divil [sic] couldn't hold her."[19]

That winter, the weather was so cold that by Christmas, the Red River around Natchitoches was frozen and the temperature was near record lows at fourteen degrees.[20] But rank did have its privileges; Birch wrote that the cold weather made it an uncomfortable Christmas for the men but that the officers "after eating a good dinner with the commanding officer…went to Town to a ball that was to have been that night but from some cause or other had been postponed, but the polite inhabitance regretting our disappointment, created in about an hour, a splendid one, at the home of a Ms. Cabbes where we passed an agreeable evening and returned to camp the next morning."[21]

For the officers, New Year's Day was again spent enjoying Natchitoches society. Birch and the other officers dined in town at the home of Captain Coombs and "after dinner the Ladies forming a cotilive [sic] party our time was spent with much pleasure and at night we all whent [sic] to a splendid ball which lasted till 2 o'clock in the morning." It was the tradition to keep the ball going once a week all winter, and it was at one of the winter balls that Captain Birch met and fell in love with Anna Ramsey, whom he would soon marry.[22]

On March 23, 1822, Major General Gains arrived at Fort Selden to discuss with Zachary Taylor the location of a post closer to the Sabine River, the new international boundary with Mexico. Taylor and Gains conducted an inspection of the surrounding territory, and Gaines, agreeing with Taylor's selection, issued Special Orders No. 19 on March 28, 1822, directing that

Lt. Col. Taylor, with the troops under his command, will, as soon as practicable occupy the position at Shield's Spring, 25 miles S. S. W. from this place; where he will canton the troops in huts of a temporary kind, sufficient for their health and comfort during the ensuing summer. The huts will be built by the troops; and to facilitate their completion, tools, wagons, and teams, planks, and nails will be furnished by the quartermaster department, upon the requisition of the immediate commanding officer.

Lt. Col. Taylor is charged with the defense of the southwestern Frontier of Louisiana; and will contribute as far as the means under his control will enable him to afford protection to the inhabitants of the interior as well as to those of the frontier.[23]

General Gaines, like so many other Americans at the time, believed that one day Texas would be the flash point in a war with Mexico. Although the Transcontinental Treaty of 1821 had set the boundary of the Louisiana Purchase at the Sabine River, many Americans were unhappy with the boundary and the treaty. Even in the United States government, there were officials claiming that the Sabine River referred to in the treaty was really the Rio Grande. There was simply too much cheap land in Texas, at a time when land prices in the United States were rising higher than most farmers could afford. Logically, the Texas land attracted waves of settlers, and it was unclear how these Americans would be treated by the new Mexican government. Hundreds of Americans had been killed or displaced fighting to free Mexico from Spain; however, not all of them were fighting for Mexican independence. Many fought to create either an independent Anglo Texas or to add Texas to the United States, and no one really knew if the Mexicans would see the Americans flocking to their territory as trying to help the young nation or as land thieves, as the Spanish had.

General Gaines reported to Adjutant General James Gadsden (later the U.S. diplomat who negotiated the Gadsden Purchase with Mexico in 1853) that:

After making due inquiry and examination of the country between this place and the Sabine river, through Lt. Col. Taylor, as well as by personal observation, I have selected a site for cantoning the troops in this quarter, which promises the advantages of health, combined with convenience or position for the protection of the settlements upon the frontier. This site is about 25 miles south-southwest from this place, upon the ridge which divides the waters of the Sabine from those of the Red River, and near the road leading from Natchitoches to the principal settlements in Texas; and not more than 18 miles upon a direct line from the Sabine River; having a constant running spring of good water (a thing seldom to be found in this country) with a dry airy ridge, and sufficient space of public land with the excellent timber, for every purpose of building and fuel for an army of twenty thousand men. The expense of and transportation from this place & Natchitoches forms the only objection to the position referred to; but this was unavoidable, as I will hereafter show.[24]

On the twenty-fourth, the General conducted a formal inspection of the troops and was pleased with what he saw:

The Commanding General is gratified to find, that notwithstanding the late afflictions of the 7th Infantry by disease and other causes, the companies at this place exhibit in their healthful appearance, their arms, equipment, and dress, and particularly in their Battalion evolutions, the most satisfactory evidence of skill and vigilant attention on the part of the immediate commandants, as well as the company officers; and of obedience and good conduct on the part of most of the Non-Commissioned Officers and private soldiers. The General congratulates the troops on the prospect of their immediately occupying an eligible position near the national boundary, where they may calculate upon the enjoyment of health and advancement in professional knowledge; and a participation in the first activity which may occur upon this important border of our country.[25]

The location that would become Fort Jesup was referred to as Shield's Spring, known for the family of squatters who lived near a natural spring located about twenty-five miles from Natchitoches and eighteen miles from the Sabine River along the Texas Road. The area was the highest ground between the Red River and the Sabine River and was the "dividing ridge" between the two waterways; all water to the east of the ridge flowed to the Red and all water to the west flowed to the Sabine. Fresh water was plentiful, not only from Shield's Spring but from numerous streams and springs located near the site. In fact, it was possible in the 1820s and 1830s to travel almost from Fort Jesup to Natchitoches by water by marching a short distance to a stream north of the post that flowed into Spanish Lake (a large, flooded area near modern-day Robeline that mostly dried up after the Red River changed course in the 1830s), which in turn flowed into the Red River about ten miles above Natchitoches. The area was well supplied with the materials needed to build the post. There were numerus outcroppings of limestone, which was used as a building material, and the soldiers established a quarry less than a mile east of the post. The region was full of large forests of pine, oak, elm and walnut trees, which not only provided building materials but were also full of wild game.[26]

On April 5, 1822, Taylor dispatched Captain Birch and three sergeants, three corporals, three musicians and fifty privates who were considered "efficient labours [*sic*]" along with "the necessary tools" to Shield's "old place" along the road between Natchitoches and Texas to begin the construction of what would one day be Fort Jesup. Birch's instructions were to build a hospital, temporary storehouses and huts for the accommodation of the soldiers. The detachment left Fort Selden on April 9 but did not arrive at Shield's Spring until the morning of the eleventh due to their overloaded baggage wagon, bad roads and having to stop to build a bridge. After pitching their tents, Birch began selecting the building sites; his men began cutting trees; and "in 27 days I erected 4 buildings 40 feet by 20, six 14 feet square, two 20 feet square, one blacksmith shop, one guard house and one hospital 50 ft. by 20." Birch referred to the post as Cantonment Shield's Spring until a permanent name could be chosen.[27]

Park volunteers raising a reproduction of an 1822-era flag. *Photo by author.*

In anticipation of the arrival of Taylor and the rest of the garrison, Captain Birch ordered on May 8, 1822, that all work be stopped until further notice for a "general police" to take place, a military term for a general cleaning and ensuring everything is returned to good order. After the general cleaning was completed, the order stated that "the men will have two or three days to wash, clean their arms, construct cooking sheds behind each set of company quarters 20 ft. x 20 ft. and to dig a "sink" (latrine) 100 yards in the rear of the quarters." Five days later, on May 13, 1822, Colonel Taylor arrived with the balance of the command from Fort Selden, and the military occupation of Fort Jesup began.[28]

CHAPTER 2

A FORT IN THE WILDERNESS

While Birch's men were constructing the first buildings, the post was referred to as Cantonment Shield's Spring; but with the official arrival of Taylor and the bulk of the command, the post was officially named Cantonment Jesup in honor of Thomas S. Jesup, quartermaster general of the U.S. Army and friend of Zachary Taylor. General Jesup was Taylor's primary mentor and political advisor in the service and was one of the few men who could control Taylor's temper. Several times during the War of 1812, Jesup convinced Taylor not to write angry (and possibly career-damaging) letters to other officers, as well as convincing him not to fight a duel with Lieutenant Colonel John McNeil of the First Infantry. Taylor also credited Jesup with helping save his rank in the reduction of the army in 1821.[29]

Even in the nineteenth century, there was no clear definition of the term *cantonment*. Starting around 1817, it began being used in the name of posts west of the Mississippi. Most of the posts that were named cantonments were "temporary" in that they were made of wood instead of stone or brick, but the term did not refer to how long the War Department planned to occupy the posts, as some cantonments were occupied for less than a year, while others would be in service for twenty or thirty years. The term also did not refer to the style of fortification, as the term was used for both posts that had wooden stockades and those that were open with no defenses, and one cantonment even had stone walls. The term would continue to be used until General Order No. 11 was issued on February

6, 1832, designating all cantonments to be renamed as forts.[30] (For the purpose of this work, the term *fort* will be used to refer to Fort Jesup from 1822 to 1832, except in quotations.)

The ridge that the fort was built on was a divide or watershed between the Sabine and Red Rivers, where rainwater flowed to the Red on one side and to the Sabine on the other. The land around Fort Jesup consisted of "a stiff, black, clayey soil." In the area were large outcroppings of limestone, which the soldiers used in mortar and other aspects of the fort's construction, establishing a quarry less than a mile to the east of the post. Also in the region were large quantities of pine, oak, elm and walnut trees, and wild game and fish were abundant. General Gaines felt that the land around Shield's Spring area could, in time of need, support a force of twenty thousand soldiers.[31]

Post surgeon Thomas Lawson described the land around Fort Jesup as "rolling and broken," writing that "along the margins of streams some good lands are found, being a black clayey soil of a tenacious nature. The high lands are covered chiefly with pine, thinly intermixed with oak and hickory; whilst the streams are skirted with beach, mulberry, sassafras, and occasionally cypress." The climate of the post was mild for a southern station, as

> the summer usually commences about the 1st of May, and continues until the last of September; during which period a high temperature, from ten o'clock until sun-set, generally prevail[s], the range of the thermometer being from 76 and 96 degrees of Fahrenheit. The nights, however, are often cool and pleasant, owing to the refreshing breezes which come in the direction of the Gulf of Mexico. What is called the rainy season begins generally in the month of February and continues until the first or middle of May. The annual quantity of rain, on an average of four years, is 47.43 inches.[32]

The first garrison in May 1822 included four companies of the Seventh Infantry: Company A, commanded by Captain (Brevet Major) David E. Twiggs; Company I, commanded by Captain J.L. Allison; Company E, commanded by Captain G. Birch; and Company D, commanded by Captain R.B. Hyde, along with surgeon Thomas Lawson (who would later be promoted to surgeon general of the Army in November 1836). The garrison was expanded when Captain Young's Company G arrived at the post in July 1822.[33]

Above: Reproduction of an 1821 infantry uniform jacket. *Photo by author.*

Left: Reproduction of an 1821 infantry hat, called a "bell crown shako" at the time. *Photo by author.*

Private Charles Martian Gray provides one of the best descriptions of the building of Fort Jesup, as well as a record of the first tragedy to take place, in his autobiography, *Old Soldier's Story*:

> *The first tree that was cut down for the purpose of erecting the Fort was an enormous pine felled by Privates Bennet, Vrisor, Bateman, and myself. Near it were a few old* markees *put up for the temporary shelter of Commissary and Quartermaster stores, and in one of them, Moses, a choice family servant of Col. Taylor's (derived through his wife, and much endeared by both master and mistress, for his intelligence, fidelity, and devotion to his owners,) had taken refuge for the purpose of enjoying a few hours repose. I informed Col. Taylor that the tree would fall upon these tents, but he paid no attention to me, especially as the other cutters were of a contrary opinion. So the cutting went on, even more briskly towards the last, then at the first, on account of the personal presence of the commanding officer. Presently this high giant of the forest fell with a momentum that made the earth tremble, in precisely an opposite direction to what was intended, tearing the tents or markees into shreds, and crushing to death Col. Taylor's faithful man Moses, who was sleeping in one of them entirely unconscious of his danger. No greater loss could have been inflicted upon Col. Taylor, for he was a most valuable slave, in all respects, and he prized him as having been received by him as a portion of his wife's dowry. But, instead of exhibiting, as many officers would have done, a great deal of ill-timed wrath at so sad an occurrence, he simply mounted the trunk of the pine, and proceeding to the spot where his noble body-servant, and really confidential friend, lay mangled and broken in every limb, exclaimed, with the most natural emotions of grief, "Boys, you have killed one of the best of men—one of the most valuable of servants,—and a servant the more highly estimated because he was the inheritance of my beloved wife."*
>
> *But the building of the Fort progressed more rapidly every day, under the systematic arrangements and intelligent control and supervision of the commanding officer. The command was divided into working parties—some designed to hew out the timbers—some to get the boards and shingles—and some to prepare the brick and mortar, —some to raise the edifice itself. I was of the party detailed to make the brick. This was a most difficult task to perform, as the men had to tread the mortar with their own feet....*
>
> *The work on the Fort and the brick-kiln went bravely on, and in the course of six or seven weeks the bricks for the Fort were all completed.*[34]

During the construction of the fort, Gray often got into mischief—or, as he called it, "playing the old soldier." While on brick detail, he "suddenly" became "ill" with "neuroligin or rheumatism of the feet" due to treading the mud in the "cool" month of April. He managed to get himself transferred to the party keeping up the fires in the brick kiln and to burn the brick, but even this lighter duty did not cure him, and he soon had an "ailment of the stomach" that could only be cured by "milk or liquor." But to get his cure, there was a double line of guards that Gray would have to slip through. So, he soon devised a plan.

There was an old woman who lived about two miles from the post on the road to Natchitoches named Mrs. Sharp, who the soldiers called Mother Sharp. She "always kept a barrel of whiskey concealed, for the accommodation of the soldiers." Gray started by taking a coffee pot to the armorer to solder the bottom of the spout closed. Next, he went to Dr. Lawson and asked for a pass to travel down the road to a farm to fill his coffee pot with fresh milk. With the pass in hand and his coffee pot in the other, he

> *proceeded, at first slowly and when out of sight, in double quick time, down the road in the direction of Mother Sharp's. Arriving at her shanty, I cried out "Good Morning, Mother Sharp!" She replies, "Ah Gray, you Devil, you are after some devilment now." "No mother Sharp I only want a gallon of whiskey put in this Coffee Pot." She hastened to her barrel, complied with my request. I then asked her to pour a little milk in the spout, which she likewise did saying "Away with you, Gray; I know now you are after some mischief."*

Gray headed back to camp, drinking "enough of John Barley Corn" to "fear no evil" but not enough to "face the Devil." He walked quickly until he was almost in sight of one of the sentinels, then he slowed and adopted "a gait, which indicated much weakness and bodily infirmity." The sentinel stopped Gray and called for the officer of the guard. When the officer arrived, he asked Gray what was in the coffee pot. Gray replied, "Nothing but a little milk, Sir, through permission of Dr. Lawson." The officer asked Gray to pour a little out of the pot, and when Gray started to pour and milk did come out, the officer let Gray pass.

Gray rushed (as fast as his "illness" would allow) to the brickyard, where he shared his "milk" with the working parties. In his words, "In about an hour's time the whole working party were drunk—some shouting and laughing —some cursing—some reelin, and some stretched insensible upon the yard, so that the idea of work had quite vanished from their minds." However, all good things must come to an end, and soon the sounds from the brickyard attracted the attention of Zachary Taylor. Taylor demanded "like a peal of thunder 'What means all this,' in tones that thrilled the nerves even of the drunken revelers." When none of the group would admit who brought the whiskey into camp, Taylor remembered the coffee pot that Gray brought into the post and demanded to see it. Gray and his friends had had the good sense to clean the pot to remove the smell of alcohol before starting their bender, but they could not remove the solder without special tools, and when Taylor saw that the holes were plugged, he ordered the entire brick party arrested and a court martial to convene the next day at eleven o'clock, consisting of Major Birch and Lieutenants Lee and Stevenson. The court found Gray guilty of unsoldierlike conduct in smuggling liquor into camp and sentenced him to do cleaning and other manual labor around the post for one month with the coffee pot strapped to him.[35]

About six or seven weeks after the "coffee pot," incident, Charles Gray was able to report to Taylor that all the bricks needed for the fort were completed and ready to be used for buildings. With his work completed, Gray felt that it was time for some relaxation and requested a pass to leave the post during the day to go fishing. His request was approved by both his company officer and Taylor. Before he set out with his friend George Riley of F Company and two Indian hunters (Choctaw Billy and his brother Red-Pepper), Gray was tempted by "the Devil or some other evil spirit" to change the pass to read "Permit Private Gray of Co. A, to leave the Fort until Retreat and to purchase a gallon of whiskey from the Sutler," even though he had sworn off alcohol after the coffee pot incident. The party set out for Beaver Lake, about two miles from the post, with the whiskey hidden under Riley's greatcoat. The group "drank, and bathed, and wrestled and caroused, the live long day"—however, they forgot to fish. As the sun began to set, the group hurried back to the post, and as they approached Taylor's quarters, the revelers tried to act as sober as possible. To their horror, Taylor stepped out of his quarters, halted the group and drew from his pocket the forged pass. Unknown to the fishing party, earlier in the day, Taylor had inspected the sutler's store and, finding the forged pass, decided to wait for Gray to return to the post. When Taylor ordered Gray to read the pass, the old soldier remembered, "My knees smote together while I did it, and despite of my desperation, I hesitated when I reached the portion added by myself, but Taylor storming at me demanded whether I could not read my own writing and when I had finally swallowed the bitter pill, [Taylor] called the Corporal of the Guard." Gray was ordered to join the other convicts sawing planks for one week. When Gray begged the Colonel that "I could not saw,—never sawed in my life,—but Col. Taylor was immovable, and insisted that I could not learn younger."[36]

In September, Zachary Taylor reported to the quartermaster general that all "timber boards, shingles, brick for the barracks…will be procured by the troops, they will cost nothing more then the Nails, Glass, Iron and the 15 cents a day to the extra duty men.…And I have no hesitation in saying that not a dollar of public money will be unnecessarily expanded at this place while I command." Charles M. Gray recalled that work continued until December 17, "when the noble structure was completed."[37]

Fort Jesup was laid out as a rectangle, with a large parade ground in the center of most of the military buildings. While the exact location and size of the buildings varied throughout the fort's existence, the post retained the same basic layout. The buildings were oriented on a northeast/southeast line that roughly followed the path of the Texas Road, instead of along a north/south line. The parade ground was a large open area where the garrison would assemble for ceremonial duties, flag raisings and lowerings, inspections and roll calls. It was also where the soldiers were drilled and trained in how to load and fire muskets and in the marching maneuvers and commands they would use in battle. On average, the soldiers who were not on guard duty or fatigue duty would spend four to six hours a day, six days a week, drilling on the parade ground.[38]

Standing on the parade ground, if one looked west toward the Texas Road, they would see a line of administrative buildings, representing the different staff departments. Each regiment, company and permanent fort had various members of the different staff departments assigned to them to ensure the smooth operation of the fort and to aid combat troops in carrying out their missions in peace and war. The staff officer who was attached to a field unit was referred to as the "assistant," and each staff department had a "general" (although their rank in most cases was colonel) who oversaw the department. While the shapes, sizes and locations of these buildings would change throughout the quarter-century history of Fort Jesup, they played a critical link in supplying the troops and supporting them in their mission of guarding the western frontier.

What would be considered "post headquarters" was the office of the post adjutant. The Adjutant-General's Department was reasonable for all the official correspondence and communications between the War

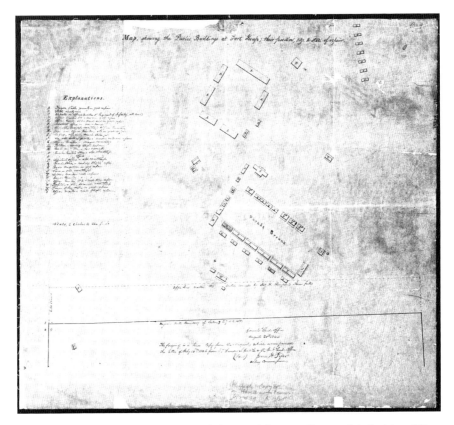

Map of Fort Jesup, 1846, showing the basic layout of the post. *Courtesy of the Louisiana Office of State Parks, Fort Jesup State Historic Site.*

Department in Washington and the widely separated forts and regiments. The department was also responsible for keeping track of the personnel files and whereabouts of all army personnel, commissioned and enlisted. Each post had an adjutant who served as an assistant to the post commander and helped him prepare and maintain the required paperwork and records. Generally, this assignment was given to a junior officer to help them learn the organizational duties of an officer. On the march, the adjutant was responsible for marking a regiment's place in line and in camp.

This row of administrative buildings also contained several warehouses (referred to as "stores"). These included storehouses for the quartermaster, commissary and ordinance. The Quartermaster's Department was overseen by Brigadier General Thomas S. Jesup, the namesake of Fort Jesup, and it was the Quartermaster's Department that supplied the army with clothing, shelter and transportation and issued food. The Quartermaster's

The parade ground today. *Photo by author.*

Department oversaw construction and maintenance of post buildings and quarters, issued uniforms and other military equipment and oversaw the transportation of food supplies. Supplying food for the army's animals and fuel for the fireplaces was also the duty of this department. Thomas Jesup would be the longest-serving quartermaster general in the history of the U.S. Army, serving from 1818 to 1860. Each post was assigned an assistant quartermaster to handle the duties of the Quartermaster's Department. It was also the duty of the assistant quartermaster to oversee the design, construction and repair of post buildings at frontier forts.

Although the quartermaster at times purchased food for the army from local sources, the purchase of bulk rations such as the hundred-pound barrels of pork, beef, flour and hard bread was the responsibility of the Subsistence Department. The Subsistence Department attempted to purchase the best-quality food at the lowest price through a bidding process for one-year contracts, in which firms and individuals agreed to supply each post with a prearranged number of rations at set times of the year. When the system broke down—as it often did, due to the firms not being able to meet their responsibilities—the local quartermasters would have to purchase food to make up for the shortfall, often at a much higher price. Regardless of which department purchased the supplies, it was the responsibility of the Quartermaster's Department to transport the supplies to the various posts or soldiers in the field and issue them. At smaller posts or larger posts short on staff officers, the duties of the Quartermaster's and Subsistence Departments were often combined.

The most popular of the administrative buildings was that of the post sutler, who provided all the items that the military did not. He was a civilian storekeeper licensed by the army to provide soliders with personal and luxury items. Usually a retired officer, the sutler was allowed a near monopoly at the post in exchange for allowing his prices to be monitored by a board of officers referred to as the council of administration and providing a percentage of his profits to the "post fund" to help cover the costs of the post's library, band and school. The Sutler's store at Fort Jesup was well stocked, but the prices were high because of the transportation costs of goods from New Orleans to Fort Jesup.[39]

Also in the line of administrative buildings was the "guardhouse." Not a jail in the way we think of a guardhouse today (although it did have cells), the guardhouse was literally a house for the guards. Each day, a group of soldiers was selected to guard the post for a twenty-four-hour period, with the size of the guard varying based on the size of the garrison. The guard was commanded by an "officer of the day," who was to oversee the guards, look after prisoners in confinement, greet visitors to the post and deal with any soldier caught coming through the line of guards without knowing the countersign or without a pass. He was to be present for each change of the guard, inspect the guards under his command and keep detailed records of any incidents during his watch. It was also the job of the officer of the day to create a sign (referred to as a "parole") and countersign that would be provided to anyone leaving the fort who would return after dark so that they could pass through the lines. The officer of the day was provided a room separate from the enlisted men to take care of his paperwork and rest when off duty. Assisting the officer of the day was the sergeant of the guard, who was personally responsible for all the enlisted members of the guard detail. Aside from being present at each changing of the guard, the sergeant and corporal of the guard were to visit each sentinel at least once an hour to ensure that they were at their posts, they were not asleep and there were no disturbances. Sergeants and corporals were to ensure that not all members of the relief detail were asleep at one time and that the noncommissioned officers were also not all asleep at one time. All members of the guard were also on the lookout for fires, as they spread quickly through a wooden garrison and could be deadly. In the event of a fire, the guard detail was to act as the fire brigade, and buckets of water were kept on hand in the guardhouse. During their tour as the guard, one-third of the men would be on station at assigned areas around the post and at a perimeter three hundred paces or more from the camp or garrison; the remainder would sleep, eat and wait in the guardhouse so that they would not disturb other soldiers during the night and would be at a central location to answer any alarms.

The most common pattern for guard duty was to spend two hours on duty and four hours off, with a new detail being posted on the even hours of eight, ten, twelve and two o'clock during the day and at night, although the length of time would be shortened during extreme weather. Soldiers on guard duty wore their dress uniforms and ensured that they were brushed and polished before reporting for duty, and they wore their uniforms for the entire twenty-four-hour period, even sleeping in their uniform with cartridge box and bayonet on (this was referred to as "sleeping in the leather"). When the guards were not on duty, their muskets were placed in a readily accessible location, and when the guards were allowed to sleep, it was on an inclined board covered in straw. While more comfortable than standing up, the "bed" prevented a deep sleep to shorten response time from the sleeping guards in the event of an emergency.[40]

The south side of the parade ground was lined by several of the soldiers' barracks. The barracks were built about six feet off the ground on stone pillars to allow for better ventilation and to protect the soldiers from "bad air" closer to the ground. The inside of the barracks was lined with a series of bunk beds that in the early nineteenth century were referred to as either "cribs" or "racks," and each bed held two soldiers on the bottom rack and two on the top rack. The barracks had racks for muskets and shelves for storing the soldiers' gear and equipment. Each company would occupy one barracks with between twenty-five and fifty soldiers per room.[41]

Behind each of the barracks was a soldiers' kitchen/mess hall where the soldiers' meals would be prepared, and the companies would eat their meals together. The army did not employ professional cooks, so each soldier would spend a month as company cook, and one enlisted man would be assigned each day as an assistant cook. In the early nineteenth century, each soldier was issued either one and a half pounds of beef or three quarters of a pound of pork, eighteen ounces of bread or flour and one gill of whisky (about four ounces). For every one hundred rations, two quarts of salt, four quarts of vinegar and one and a half pounds of candles were issued. Twice a week, fresh meat was to be substituted for salted meat.

Reproduction bunk in a display at Fort Jesup SHS. *Photo by author.*

The *General Regulations for the Army, 1825* provided guidelines:

201. Bread ought not to be burnt, but baked to an equal brown colour. The crust ought not to be detached from the crum. On opening it, when fresh, one ought to smell a sweet and balsamic odour.

202. The troops ought not to be allowed to eat soft bread fresh from the oven, without first toasting it. This process renders it nearly as wholesome and nitrous as stale bread.

203. Fresh meat ought not to be cooked before it has had time to bleed and to cool; and meats will generally be boiled, with a view to soup; sometimes roasted or baked but never fried....

205. To make soup, put into the vessel at the rate of five pints of water to a pound of fresh meat; apply a quick heat, to make it boil promptly; skim off the foam, and then moderate the fire; salt is then put in, according to the palate. Add the vegetables of the season one or two hours, and sliced bread some minutes before the simmering is ended. When the broth is sensibly reduced in quantity, that is, after five or six hours' cooking, the process will be complete.[42]

Located about one hundred yards behind the soldiers' barracks was the post's hospital. While medical care in the early nineteenth century was primitive compared to modern standards, army doctors had higher levels of training then many of their civilian counterparts. Fort Jesup was blessed with an up-to-date hospital (for the era) and some of the best doctors on the frontier. In fact, two of the post's doctors were later promoted to surgeon general of the army. With no microscopes, X-rays or other modern technologies, doctors of the nineteenth century were forced to base treatments on observations of systems. Diseases were thought to be caused by bad blood, "miasmas" (bad air from swamps or from decaying materials) or sudden changes in temperature. Bloodletting was still a common practice, in which amounts of blood were removed to allow the body to return to balance and/or produce

Soldiers' kitchen with the ruins of the pillars that the soldiers' barracks were built on. *Photo by author.*

Inside of the soldiers' kitchen, arranged as it may have appeared in the late 1830s. *Photo by author.*

Open-hearth cooking in the soldiers' kitchen. *Photo by author.*

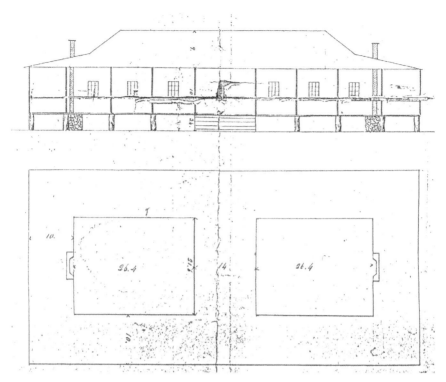

Plan of one of the hospitals at Fort Jesup. *Courtesy of the Louisiana Office of State Parks, Fort Jesup State Historic Site.*

good blood. Bloodletting did little to fight illness, but it did have the effect of lowering the temperature, leading doctors to believe it was helping cure the body. Fort Jesup was one of the healthiest posts on the western frontier; however, there were still many diseases (diarrhea and dysentery being the most common, with 1,392 cases) and approximately seventy soldiers died from diseases (roughly 3 percent of the troops stationed there).[43]

On the opposite side of the parade ground from the enlisted barracks were the officers' quarters. While dozens of enlisted men might have occupied each barracks, only a few officers shared the officers' quarters buildings. Two lieutenants were assigned to share two rooms, a captain was allowed two rooms to himself and the number of rooms increased with higher ranks. As a general rule, one room was set up as a bedroom and one as a parlor/sitting area. As most officers were from the middle class, the amount and quality of the furnishings in their homes were much higher than in the enlisted men's quarters.[44]

Reproduction medical tools. *Photo by author.*

Many of the officers were married, and their wives and children often lived with them on post, allowing them to maintain household and family life. Officers were also allotted a certain number of servants, based on their rank, that the army would provide pay, food and lodging for. Some of these servants were the wives of enlisted men, some were men and women trying to find employment on the frontier and some were enslaved persons. A third group of women at the post were the laundresses employed by the army at the rate of four per company. While these laundresses may not have been models of female virtue, they were not women of low moral character, as they are sometimes portrayed. In fact, their conduct and behavior were subject to military regulations, and if she became a distraction, a laundress could be dismissed.[45]

Left: Pitcher recovered from the site of one of the officer's quarters. *Right*: Teacup recovered from the site of one of the officer's quarters. *Photos by author.*

With most of the construction completed, Fort Jesup could turn its attention to its more military duties. Patrols were sent into the old No Man's Land and to the Sabine River, supplies were transported between the post and Natchitoches and soldiers not needed for other duties were drilled on the parade ground an average of six hours a day, six days a week. Fort Jesup was a rare post on the frontier that had a large enough garrison to not only provide soldiers for duties necessary to keep the men alive (cutting firewood, tending gardens, cooking, and so on)—but the garrison was large enough that there were almost always squads and companies present for drill and able to maintain at least some of their military bearing, unlike many smaller posts, where soldiers spent so much time on work details that they were barely able to march, load a musket or know what to do in an emergency.

Nineteenth-century armies were divided into three main combat branches, each with a different role in battle. Artillery used canons to weaken fortifications and to break the morale of troops in the field. Cavalry were mounted troops used to scout for the army, to encircle retreating enemies and to try to break through weakened sections of formation. For most of its existence, Fort Jesup would be an infantry post. Because most of the artillery

Above: Park volunteers portraying laundresses. *Photo by author.*

Left: Plate recovered from the site of one of the officers' quarters. *Photo by author.*

Opposite, top: Diagram of an American six-pound cannon. *Courtesy of the Louisiana Office of State Parks, Fort Jesup State Historic Site.*

Opposite, bottom: Six-pound iron cannon ball. *Photo by author.*

regiments were needed to garrison the coastal forts with the heavy cannons, frontier infantry units were also trained in field artillery tactics. The level of training varied from post to post based on the availability of artillery rounds and the attention of the commander. General Gains reported that the soldiers at Fort Jesup were "little acquainted with artillery duty" beyond firing the cannons, which still put them ahead of some forts, which could not even find the right-size cannon ball for their cannons. In 1824, the fort was outfitted with 4 four-pounder cannons, 2 three-pounder cannons and 2 twenty-four-pounder cannons (named for the weight of the cannon balls they fired). The 1834 ordinance report listed 5 six-pound field cannons, 3 six-pound

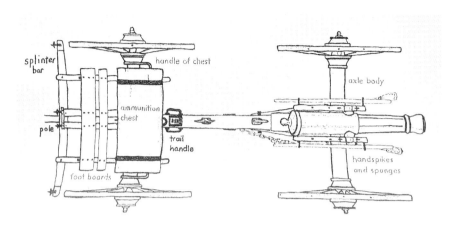

splinter bar

handle of chest

axle body

pole

ammunition chest

trail handle

handspikes and sponges

foot boards

light cannons and 2 twenty-four-pound cannons on garrison carriages, as well as 511 pounds of powder, 1,093 musket cartridges and primes, 356 loose canister shells, 200 rounds of fixed shot, 184 six-pound shells and 1,067 rounds of grapeshot. Also in the storehouses was an assortment of supplies, which included flax, flannel, thread, tow, twine, brass, scrap metal, beeswax, glue, pitch, tar, harnesses, lead, lacquer, oil, turpentine, German steel, one compass, several pieces of ivory and 100 pounds of rope.[46]

While George Birch and his men were constructing the post, other soldiers were put to work bringing order and law to No Man's Land. Almost twenty years of lawlessness and lack of government control had created a situation where criminals, squatters and smugglers had flooded the area. Compounding the problem was that many of the settlers were loyal to Spain, not the United States. The region around Spanish Lake, which is located a few miles north of modern-day Robeline, was one of the many areas with a large Spanish population. The residents were the descendants of the Spanish settlers and soldiers of Los Adaes, which had been the capital of the province of Texas from 1729 to 1770. After the Spanish ordered the abandonment of the mission and fort at Los Adaes, the settlers first traveled to San Antonio; however, many felt that conditions were so bad that they petitioned to be able to return to their former homes. Several settlers traveled as far as east Texas, establishing Nacogdoches, Texas, and some returned to Spanish Lake. Unsure of the loyalty of the Spanish residents living along the main waterway between Fort Jesup and Natchitoches, which ran through Spanish Lake, Taylor established a camp at Spanish Lake of one corporal and three privates to keep an eye on the population. Although the population never revolted against the United States, Mexican agents such as Manual Flores repeatedly attempted to stir the population against the Americans.[47]

In July, Taylor was transferred back to the First Infantry, but the order did not take effect immediately; he remained at Fort Jesup until November 9, 1822, when he left for his new post at Cantonment Robertson, outside of Baton Rouge. The fort's new commander, Lieutenant Colonel James B. Many, arrived in Natchitoches on November 30. James Many was a native of Delaware who received his commission as a lieutenant in the engineers on June 4, 1798. He soon transferred to the artillery, where he served for several years in the Northeast. Following the Louisiana Purchase of 1803, he was sent to the Southwest to take command of Arkansas Post, a former French outpost on the juncture of the Arkansas and Mississippi Rivers. He served with distinction in the War of 1812, and with the end of the war, he was given command of Fort St. Phillip on the Mississippi River below New Orleans with a promotion to major of the Fourth Regiment of Artillery. During the army reorganization of 1821, Many was first sent to the Fourth Infantry, then to the Fifth Infantry and finally to the Seventh Infantry (all in the course of less than a year).[48]

By 1823, Fort Jesup was the largest military post in the state of Louisiana, with four companies stationed at the fort and one company on detached service at Cantonment Taylor, totaling about 206 officers and men (each company had between 47 and 53 men). Fort Jesup surpassed even the garrisons at New Orleans (the state capital until 1848) and Baton Rouge. The 1823 "Annual Estimate of Funds and Supplies" for the quartermaster's department requested funds to buy supplies for 17 officers (2 field and staff, 5 captains, 10 subalterns), 255 enlisted men, 15 washwomen, 3 servants, 3 horses, 4 mules and 8 oxen. In October 1824, a detachment of recruits from the Natchez, Mississippi recruiting station arrived at Fort Jesup numbering 58 men (60 men left the recruiting station, but two were confined by the civil authority in Natchez), as well as the first local recruit, Private James Fox of Natchitoches. In April 1823, the garrison was increased from five companies to seven companies, with the addition of Company G, under Captain Young, and Company H, under the command of Captain Davenport.[49]

For the rest of the 1820s, soldiers from Fort Jesup would lay the groundwork for western expansion by mapping the region, building roads, clearing the region's rivers and opening them for navigation, bringing law and order to the former Neutral Strip and protecting settlers and travelers on the Texas Road. They would hone their military skills on the parade ground while growing their own food and building and repairing their own quarters. All the while, the officers and soldiers were blazing a trail for Americans wishing to start a new life on the western frontier.

CHAPTER 3

THE TRAILBLAZERS

Without the soldiers who called frontier forts home, western migration and settlement would not have been possible. These soldiers built roads through the wilderness and created maps of unexplored regions. Frontier commanders were charged with exploring and mapping the regions around their forts and identifying important natural resources (such as fur-producing animals, crop land and so forth), water sources for both drinking and waterpower and any other resource that would be helpful for settlement or for supporting large bodies of troops in time of need. By the 1840s, a person could travel overland from the Great Lakes to the Sabine River on roads built by soldiers, opening these regions to floods of settlers.

When the Mexican government opened Mexican Texas to American immigration in April 1823, word quickly spread through the United States about the "promised land" of Texas, starting a wave of migration as hundreds of settlers moved along the old El Camino Real, which Americans now called the San Antonio Trace, the Road to Mexico or the Texas Road. Fort Jesup became an important waystation and resupply point for weary travelers, many camping in the vicinity of the fort and some visiting the officers and staying in the garrison. One such party that visited the fort on its way to Texas in 1824 was that of Judge Henry A. Bullard and the Reverend Timothy Flint. Reverend Flint, who graduated from Harvard in 1800, had moved to Louisiana in 1823 to become the principal of the Rapide Seminary in Alexandria. He later wrote a book about his travels, in which he described the fort and its officers:

We were most hospitably welcomed at "Cantonment Jesup" a post within twenty-five miles of the Sabine, and situated the fartherest [sic] to southwest of any in the United States. They have very comfortable quarters, two companies of soldiers, and a number of very gentlemanly officers, the whole under the command of Col. Many. The water from the southern extremity of the esplanade falls into the Sabine, and from the northern, into the Red River. It is of course the highest point between the two rivers. It produced singular sensations, to see all the pomp and circumstance of military parade, and to hear the notes of the drum and fife, breaking the solitude of the wilderness of the Sabine. By this garrison passes the great road to the crossing on the Sabine. Beyond that river the forest country continues thirty miles. Then commences the vast prairies, that reach to the Passo del Norte. The road from Sabine to Mexico is said to be very good, passable with carriages, and the worst part of the distance, in the valley of MEXICO, within a short distance of that city. The passing is already considerable. Many of the young men of our region have made excursions to that city. It is easy to see that the improving spirt of the age, even in the Mexican country, will soon make this a stage and a mail route.[50]

Although it is difficult to determine the exact number of settlers who chose to travel the overland route past Fort Jesup, it is safe to assume that the number is in the thousands. In the first decade of immigration to Texas, roughly thirty-three thousand settlers migrated to Texas, settling mostly in the East, and one of the most common and least expensive routes was the overland route down the Texas Road. There was also an unknown number of merchants (American and Mexican) who traveled back and forth over the road. During the Mexican era and the early republic period of Texas, Natchitoches was the favorite trading post of Texas, and most of the overland trade into Texas was along the San Antonio Trace. Protecting these settlers and travelers and maintaining the road to Texas would be a major duty of the soldiers of the fort.[51]

Another responsibility commanders of frontier forts were charged with was exploring and mapping the region around their posts to identify possible routes for roads, natural resources and defendable positions in the event of invasion. In the summer of 1823, Colonel Many led an expedition to explore and map the Sabine River. He selected Captain Hyde, Sergeant Bateman and twelve privates, including Charles M. Gray. These explorers set out for Gaines Crossing around the middle of the Sabine River (near the site of modern-day Pendleton Bridge), run by General Gaines's brother. Once they reached the site, they built what Gray called "the Ark" to carry themselves and their supplies down the river. On their journey, they encountered bears, wolves, wildcats, catamounts (a term used to describe mid-size to large wild cats, such as cougars), deer and wild turkeys. Gray recalled that "at night, the growling of the bears, the howling of the wolves, and the screams of the American panther, made the hair of the sturdiest soldiers stand on end." The little party found a landscape full of all types of vegetation and "so teeming with insects of every variety, that animal life abounded there to an exuberance never before witnessed. The canes were like small saplings, the swamps were like dark clouds, and the wilderness was made alive by the ten thousand birds of every hue, reptiles of every class, and beasts of every name, that sported, and crept, and roamed, and fed, and procreated, in its broad and prolific bosom."

The "brave band" of explorers reached Sabine Lake on July 3 and celebrated the Fourth of July hunting deer, fishing and "in reveling, in singing patriotic and war songs, in feasting, in drinking, and in the most glorious jollification." Apparently, James Many, "a soldier, and a gentleman of the old school…had no hesitation in ministering occasionally to the weakness of human nature, issued that day to his detachment three extra gills of whiskey." The next day:

> the party started for the mouth of the Kulkasue River, distant about 30 miles, which they reached before sun-down, although they took time to supply themselves with a plenty of venisoin [sic] and other nice game on the voyage. Having surveyed this River in the course of three days, the detachment issued from their Ark, anchored it, left it to the tender mercies of the savage, of the wild beasts, and of the winds and the waves, and set their Compass, and began their route in an overland march for Fort Jesup.
>
> Though this exploration had lasted for forty days, during which we had never heard a cock crow, or seen a human face, and had been surrounded eternally with the denizens of the forest, yet no accident had happened to a single man, and no man even suffered from a day's severe indisposition. So was the return to Fort Jesup, through the wilderness, which lasted for eight days, altogether fortunate and successful, without any mishap or loss of course or distance.[52]

Beginning in 1825, the soldiers would be called on to fight a different kind of battle, but not against another army—this would be a battle against nature. This battle would help open North Louisiana, East Texas and

Oklahoma to settlement and would lead to the founding of one of the major cities in Louisiana. Steamboat travel began on the Red River in early 1820 when the steamboat *Yonker* docked at Alexandria, Louisiana, on January 27. Beginning in March, regular steamer service was established between Alexandria and New Orleans; later that month, the run was extended to Natchitoches, taking about six days and three hours. By 1825, there were seven steamboats working the Red River, and all the captains were eager to expand their business farther upstream into Texas and Arkansas, but they were blocked by a large obstruction called the "Great Raft."

Above Natchitoches, the Red River was blocked by a series of logjams composed of decayed logs, shrubs and soil that had broken lose upstream and become entangled. They were named "rafts" by explorer Thomas Freeman in 1806 because, unlike a log snag in most western rivers, these log snags drifted slowly downriver, crashing into each other and becoming larger and more entangled. During times of high water, shallow-draft keelboats could navigate through the obstruction at a speed of about three miles an hour, averaging about twenty-one miles a day, but for most of the year, the settlers upriver and the garrison at Fort Towson were cut off from river transport. Not only did the raft prevent navigation, but the annual flooding also covered hundreds of acres of rich farmland that settlers wanted open to plant cotton, corn, tobacco and vegetables. Starting in 1825, the General Assembly of the Territory of Arkansas sent a petition to Congress requesting that the main channel of the river be cleared at least as far as the mouth of the Kiamichi. The legislature justified the request by stating that neither the white settlers nor the Native tribes living above Sulphur Fork had regular access to supplies.

Colonel Many was directed to dispatch a team of officers to investigate the Red River and determine if it would be feasible to clear the channel for navigation. Many selected Captain George Birch and Lieutenant Lee, along with a detachment of soldiers, for the expedition, which lasted about two months. Upon their return, Colonel Many sent a report to the president of the United States, the governor of Louisiana and the *Natchitoches Courier*, one of the newspapers published in Natchitoches, which published the report on March 13, 1826. Many reported that in the one hundred miles above Natchitoches, there were 181 different logjams, ranging from ten yards to a half mile in length. While Colonel Many did not say that it would be impossible to clear the raft, he did report that "to clear these obstructions would be a tremendous and expensive task." The colonel also suggested that it may be more advantageous to clear the Sabine River, mindful of the "trying times, such as exists between ourselves and our neighbors to the west." For the next decade, soldiers from Forts Jesup and Towson would work to keep the river open to navigation, proving the economic importance of the steamboat trade on the Red River.[53]

The year 1826 saw one of the first armed conflicts between settlers in Texas and the Mexican government, and as with so many conflicts in Texas, some of Fort Jesup's soldiers would find themselves involved. Charles Martin Gray recalled in his *Old Soldier's Story* that upon their return from the Sabine River, "all things went on well—all were happy, contented, well-fed, well-clad, well-drilled, and well cared for." But in late 1826, there was a loud disturbance one night, and Captain Young threatened the severest punishment allowed when he found the perpetrators. A "worthless soldier by the name of Brady" accused Gray of being one of the soldiers involved in the disturbance. Not sure if his captain would believe that he was innocent, Gray decided to head to Texas to join Colonel Edwards's revolt. Gray "invested myself with my very best appearance and taking the Mexican Road: proceeding via Gains crossing, reached Nacogdoches."[54]

Nacogdoches was in open revolt when Gray arrived. Stephen F. Austin was the most successful of the empresarios, but he was not the only one. When Mexico opened Texas to settlement in 1824, they licensed several other empresarios to bring settlers into Texas, including Haden Edwards. The Edwards tract was located north of Austin's colony near Nacogdoches. All empresarios were required to honor existing land claims, but most empresarios only had a few claims to deal with because of where their colonies were located. Edwards's colony was located in an area that had been settled since the late eighteenth century by Spanish subjects. During the years of the Mexican Revolution, many Americans had also settled near Nacogdoches, and while there were some "wholesome" settlers, many were squatters, drifters, smugglers, debtors and felons who saw little reason to work with Edwards and the new settlers. Edwards did little to endear himself to the older settlers when he posted notices in town during the fall of 1825 that all current settlers must show proof of their claims; if they did not prove their legal claim, Edwards would sell their land without notice. This notice immediately created a rift between the old settlers and the newcomers, and the rift would continue to grow.

When the time came for the election of the alcalde (a combination of sheriff and mayor), the town split into two camps. Edwards put forward Chrichester Chaplin, who was not trusted by the older settlers because he was not only a newcomer but was also married to Edwards's daughter. The older settlers supported Sam Norris, but when the votes were counted, Chaplin won. Further angering the old settlers was the fact that Edwards was the vote counter. The older settlers quickly appealed the election to Governor Saucedo at San Antonio, who overturned the election. Edwards took the decision as a personal insult, objected to the interference in local affairs by the governor and refused to turn over the office. The old settlers threated to take the office by force, if necessary, and Edwards finally backed down. However, Edwards and his brother had so vilified the state government and Saucedo that the government canceled his grant.

Now, the new settlers were outraged, as they had no clear title to their lands without Edwards's grant and stood to lose everything. Edwards also stood to lose over $50,000 (roughly $1.5 million in today's dollars) in lost time, resources and capital. To save their investments, the newcomers organized a militia, arrested Norris and one of his supporters and seized the government building in town. They also made alliances with some of the Cherokee leaders in the region who were also upset at the state government.[55]

Gray arrived in town and soon enlisted in the milia, where he was quickly outfitted as a "Freedonian, the name which Col. Edwards saw proper to designate his party." Gray soon encountered his friend George Riley, who had deserted the post a few days before Gray without Gray's knowledge. Unlike Gray, who had deserted for fear of punishment, Riley deserted for the adventure the Fredonian Rebellion offered. Not long after Gray arrived, the rebellion began falling apart. The Mexicans sent a force of several hundred soldiers from San Antonio, the Cherokee did not rise up as hoped and—worst of all for the rebellion—Stephen F. Austin sided with the Mexican government and sent militia from his colony to put down the revolt. Outnumbered, Edwards and his supporters fled to the United States in January 1827. Gray and Riley also fled town with the others but got lost along the way and spent a few weeks wandering in the forest until they came across some friendly Indians, who not only fed them but also helped them reach the house of Choctaw Billy, who was often employed as a scout at Fort Jesup. Choctaw Billy was able to lead them back to the post. Instead of the punishment for desertion that they feared, "the two adventurous soldiers of Freedonia were returned to their duty, without punishment, sleeping that night a sounder, sweeter sleep, then they had ever slept before since the days of their dear childhood."[56]

Things may have ended well for Gray and Riley, but the Fredonian Rebellion forever poisoned the water between the colonists and the Mexican government. The rebellion was only led by about fifteen men, but it caused the Mexicans to conclude that the Fredonians had plans to add Texas to the United States. Even though Austin's colony had remained loyal to the Mexican government and even sent troops to help put down the revolt, the incident caused Mexican officials to become increasingly suspicious of all Anglo-Americans, and relations between colonists and the Mexican government would worsen for the next eight years.

In March 1827, Major General Edmund P. Gaines, commander of the Western Department of the Army, inspected Cantonment Jesup and reported that

> *Cantonment Jesup stands on the top of the ridge which divides the waters of the Red River from those of the Sabine twenty-five miles to the westward of Natchitoches, upon the road leading from that city to Nacogdoches. It is one of the most healthful and elevated positions of the interior of Louisiana, amply supplied with pure water, with an abundance of timber for fuel and building. The adjacent land is principally deemed to be public property, and though generally too poor for several miles around to attract the attention of speculators, it affords tolerable gardens and fields for corn and pasturage. A position near the Sabine River, from twenty to twenty-five miles further westward, if equally healthy, would be better adapted to the immediate charge of the western frontier bordering on Texas; but it is believed that no part of that frontier has proven so healthy as the position now occupied.*
>
> *Police: Very good, generally, and in some respects exemplary; barracks not as airy as I deem to be desirable in this climate for the summer, and though originally well built with logs in the ordinary way, their roofs are now beginning to decay and leak, and they cannot be fit for use more than for a year or two longer without extensive repairs.*[57]

Fort Towson (originally referred to as Cantonment Towson and named for Paymaster General Nathan Towson) was founded in April 1824 near the Kiamichi River by two companies of the Seventh Infantry, one from Fort Jesup and the other from the garrison at Sulfur Fork under Major Alexander Cummings. The purpose of the new fort was to help regulate trade between white settlers and the Indians, as well as to prevent illegal slave trading. To supply Forts Jesup and Towson, goods and supplies were purchased by quartermaster agents in Philadelphia, New York, Washington and New Orleans, then sent to Natchitoches, where soldiers from Fort Jesup would collect the supplies for their fort and transport the remaining supplies to Fort Towson. Although water transportation was preferred because it made it possible to carry larger loads faster and cheaper, the Red River route was not ideal. It was over six hundred miles by water between the forts and only open to navigation for about five months out of the year. Boats had to navigate through logjams and over sandbars upstream against the current.

To ease the supply problems, and to reinforce and secure the frontier and its lines of communication, Congress and the War Department authorized the building of a road between the two posts in 1827. The roads the soldiers cut out of the wilderness were called Military Road No. 10 (from Cantonment Towson to the northern boundary of Louisiana about 186 miles) and Military Road No. 11 (from the boundary of Louisiana to Natchitoches about 76 miles), for a total of roughly 262 miles through heavily forested areas. Military Road No. 11 entered Louisiana in the extreme northwest corner of present-day Claiborne Parish and ran toward present-day Minden, then through Campti and Grand Ecore and, finally, into the town of Natchitoches. To complete the network of roads, Military Road No. 13 connected Cantonment Towson to Fort Smith (near Little Rock) and Fort Gibson, Oklahoma.

To build this impressive system of roads through the wilderness, the soldiers spent six months living in cramped tents, working in all the extremes of weather. For each crossing, the soldiers would have to either wade across the creeks or stand in the water as they built bridges in wool uniforms. They were constantly having to help pull wagons that got stuck out of the mud. Every inch of the road had to be cleared by hand. Trees had to be cut down and then dragged out of the way. Stumps had to be dug out or burned, and then the ground had to be smoothed out. Bridges had to be constructed over creeks and marshes, which meant that soldiers had to stand in the water to position the timbers and supports, no matter the temperature. Work on the road was so difficult that even Charles Gray had little time or energy to play his usual tricks and he recalled that the soldiers were too tired "to perform any extra tricks, or even to expend any surplus wit and humor." While this road was important to the military, it's role as the main north–south land route west of the Mississippi cannot be overlooked. When this section of road was added to the other sections built by soldiers from other frontier posts, it was possible to travel by land from Fort Jesup to the Great Lakes and allowed for the opening of more regions for settlement and allowed goods to be transported to markets.[58]

Building the road left Charles Gray with a "thirst for liquor." While most of the garrison was occupied building the road, several whiskey peddlers set up a shop four miles from the fort. Gray may have had a thirst for alcohol, but he and Riley had no money to buy whiskey, so Gray came up with a plan. Gray gave Riley his greatcoat to trade for the whiskey and a five-gallon keg and sent him ahead. Gray "procured another coat, and an officer's sword, and a drum cord" and arranged to arrive at Brown's cabin after the keg was filled. Seeing that the keg was full, Gray burst into the house and

> *imitated the performance of a young domineering officer to the letter. I cursed Riley, and cursed Brown. I strode across the floor and asked them if they did not know it was contrary to the Army Regulations to traffic in whiskey so near the Garrison. I demanded of Brown, if he did not know he was also violating Louisiana law, in selling liquor without a license. And also accusing Riley of having stolen my over-coat and sold it, I withdrew from my pocket the drum cord, and tied him hard and fast, while he was all the time begging as if in imminent peril of his life.*

By this point, Brown was convinced that Gray might very well do physical harm to both him and Riley, and Brown began begging the "lieutenant" for forgiveness, agreeing to return the greatcoat and even offering to give Gray a barrel of whiskey for the use of the hospital. Gray quickly took Brown up on the offer, and Gray and Riley carried the barrel back to the fort. Years of trying to sneak illegal whiskey into the post had taught them many lessons, and this time, they were not only able to slip it past the guards without being caught but were also able to hide the barrel and enjoy its contents without being detected.[59]

There were few violent conflicts between soldiers and tribes in the 1820s; however, the troops from Fort Jesup were involved in at least one skirmish. The quiet of the garrison was broken when the post received word that the Comanches were "making hostile demonstrations upon Fort Towson." A relief column was quickly assembled, composed of forty men selected from all the companies—including Charles Gray— under the command of Captain George Birch. The detachment arrived at Fort Towson after a forced march of eight days and nights, carrying all their supplies on their backs. A few days after the party arrived, musician Glenn, Corporal Gloyd and Private Clark went about a mile and a quarter from Fort Towson to fish. A few minutes after the party left the garrison, Glenn and Gloyd were shot down by arrows. Clark, who was in the rear, took the alarm back to the fort. Lieutenant Page was sent with a detachment of troops and the Indian scout known as Caddo Billy. The next morning, Caddo Billy signed that the enemy was nearby. Lieutenant Page put his forces in the line of battle and, as Gray recalled,

> *their old priming was replaced with new, and fresh powder, and under cover of the under-growth, they were directed to proceed on their hands and their feet until they came within point-blank distance of the enemy, present their pieces, each at his man, and at the discharge of the Caddo's rifle, deliver a general fire. When they approached within fair view of the camp, a most horrid and dreadful scene presented itself, especially to me. The Indians were drunk and unwary. The evening and the day before, they had killed all the settlers—men, women, and children,—within the vicinity of the Fort; and the last they had killed were esquire Bowman, wife and daughter, he being an old Indian trader, as well as a kind of Sutler for the Soldiers, although living nine miles off, on the road to Fort Jesup. Here they had obtained their liquor, for Bowman kept a still and it was this that brought down upon their heads so sharply and suddenly, the retributive justice that followed their diabolical acts of cruelty. They had erected in the center of their camp a long pole, on which was strung forty-five scalps, of men, women, and children. Around this, they were singing and dancing, with savage glew [sic], while their meat and corn were being cooked in several large pots that were on the fire boiling. At the head of the pole, was the scalp of poor old Bowman, next that of his wife, and then followed the scalp of the beautiful Mary Bowman, their daughter, with long auburn ringlets, which had not yet lost their golden line, though bedabbled and bedraggled with her own blood, and the blood of her father and mother.*
>
> *At this appalling sight, my heart rose to my very throat cloaking me with sorrow and rage. Oft had I seen Mary Bowman, in all the pride of her youth and beauty, and having frequently to carry the express from Fort Jesup to Fort Towson, and stop at her father's house, I had become not only an acquaintance, but a devoted lover of hers. Indeed she was the toast of all the gallant soldiers—officers and men,—then stationed in the far West. As there were few or no young women in the wilderness wild, but herself, she shone like a bright sport—a green oasis in the desert, a brilliant star in a firmament of eternal night. In an instant, though, as before remarked, I recognized her very scalp by her golden wavy locks, and I had recovered a little from the first shock it produced upon my nerves, I felt I could charge into a whole Regiment of the Red Devils, and put them all to death with my own hands. Fear was banished from my heart, and I longed for nothing so much as the signal to fire, and then to dash upon the murderous hellish*

fiends, who were dancing and carousing over the reeking scalp of my sweet angel, who was as pure, in life, "as the icicle that curdled in frost, from purest snow, and hung on Dian's temple."

At length, after we had approached, unobserved to within sixty or seventy yards of the painted demons, the old Caddo leveled his rifle, and at its quick, sharp, and dreadful crack, forty muskets were discharged right into the thick crowd of the drunken frolicking Indians, and with a shout and fixed bayonets, the whites then charged upon them. Such a scampering was there then for dear life by Big Buffalo, Pigeon Wing, Black Snake, Little Turtle, Tiger Skin, Deer Head, and Bald Eagle, as was never before witnessed on grand prairie, or on any other part of this broad earth. Our men, had killed nine of them outright, at the first fire, and the number of wounded they could not tell, for miserable cowards flew through the plains, and although, there were twenty trails of blood issuing from the horrid camp, they could never overtake another Indian. There were at least sixty or an hundred of those Yellow Skins, and only an hour before, under the influence of whiskey and their demoniac passions, they were boasting of their exploits, in taking the lives of helpless women and children, but when they came to be confronted with men, having arms in their hands, their mean sneaking souls, betook them to panic, and to utter rout and confusion.[60]

Once the situation on the frontier settled down, the detachment returned to Fort Jesup to resume the monotony of garrison and fatigue duties.

With the passing of the Indian Removal Act in 1830, plans were made to transfer the Cherokee, Choctaw, Creek, Chickasaw and Seminoles, plus numerous smaller tribes, to lands west of the Mississippi River and to create the "Permanent Indian Frontier," guarded by a line of forts running from Fort Jesup in the south to Fort Snelling in Minnesota. The act would also cause the War Department to shift soldiers to new positions and reinforce key posts along the new frontier. Fort Jesup was no exception, as it was decided to relocate the troops of the Seventh Infantry to their regimental headquarters at Fort Gibson in the Indian Territory. In March 1830, Many was ordered to Fort Gibson to prepare for the transfer of the Seventh to the Indian Territory.[61] Because of the act, Fort Jesup would gain an elevated status as a regimental headquarters with the arrival of the Third United States Infantry, but the Indian Removal Act would lead to the suffering of tens of thousands Native Americans on forced marches to their new homes and would eventually lead to the longest Indian war in American history. Even though it was fought hundreds of miles from Fort Jesup, the men of the garrison would be drawn into the conflict, and many would pay the ultimate sacrifice.

CHAPTER 4

EXPANSION, REPAIRS AND THE FOUNDING OF SHREVEPORT AND LAKE CHARLES

W hen Colonel Many and the Seventh Infantry companies at Fort Jesup were ordered to join the rest of the Seventh Infantry at their headquarters at Fort Gibson (located in modern-day central Oklahoma), they were replaced by Brevet Brigadier General Henry Leavenworth with six companies of the Third United States Infantry; the post also became the headquarters for the Third Infantry. While most of the Third Infantry's first years at Fort Jesup would be spent repairing buildings and roads, trying to clear the Red River of logjams and performing the typical garrison duties and drills, they were involved in several events that helped open more of Louisiana to settlement, and eventually, they would be called to put their training to the test as war clouds gathered on the frontier.

The Third Regiment of United States Infantry was originally founded on March 5, 1792, as part of the expansion of the army to protect the frontier, which at that time was the Ohio River Valley. During this era, the army was organized as the Legion of the United States, and each of the four "sub legions" was a combined arms unit with its own infantry, artillery and mounted units, able to deal with any emergency on the isolated frontier. Even though the legion model had been highly successful under General "Mad" Anthony Wayne at the Battle of Fallen Timbers, in 1796, the army was reorganized on more traditional lines, and the Infantry of the Third Sub Legion became the Third Regiment of Infantry. With the election of President Jefferson, the military budget was cut, and the Third, along with all but two infantry regiments and a few artillery units, was discharged in

1802. A few years later, as the possibility of war with Great Britain increased, the military was enlarged, and the Third was reactivated in 1808. The unit served with distinction during the War of 1812, fighting with Andrew Jackson at the Battle of Horse Bend on March 25, 1814, and Pensacola on November 7, 1814. In the postwar reorganization of the army, the Third was consolidated with the Second, Seventh and Forty-Fourth to form a new First Infantry, and a new Third Infantry was created by consolidating the First, Seventeenth, Twenty-Fourth, Twenty-Eighth and Thirtieth. For the next eleven years, the regiment guarded the Great Lakes region, until they were ordered to Missouri in 1826 to establish Jefferson Barracks. In September 1831, the headquarters of the regiment was moved to Fort Jesup, along with Companies B, D, F and H.[62]

The post's new commander, Brevet Brigadier General Henry Leavenworth, was a distinguished officer who had seen action in the War of 1812 and in several Indian campaigns. He was also involved in the construction of several key posts, including Camp Coldwater (which later became Fort Snelling), Fort Leavenworth and Jefferson Barracks. Leavenworth was born on December 10, 1783, in New Haven, Connecticut, the youngest of seven children of Jesse Leavenworth, who was the colonel of a Connecticut regiment during the American Revolution. His grandfather, Thomas Leavenworth, was a medical doctor who immigrated to New England from Great Britain. As a young child, his father left his mother, Catherine Frisbee Leavenworth, and moved the children to Danville, Vermont. As a young man, Henry moved to Delhi, New York, and began studying law in the office of Revolutionary veteran and general in the state militia Erastus Root. Root was also involved in state politics, holding offices in both the state assembly and U.S. Congress. Leavenworth was admitted to the New York bar as a lawyer in 1804, quickly became involved in state politics and was elected captain of the local militia company. The next year, in 1805, Leavenworth married Elizabeth Morrison, and they had two children, Eunice and Jesse, but the marriage ended in divorce. Henry was remarried in 1810 to the seventeen-year-old Electa Knapp, but she died in childbirth. In 1813, Henry married Harriet Lovejoy, and they had a daughter, Alida.

Commissioned a captain at the beginning of the War of 1812, Leavenworth would fight in several key battles along the Canadian border. During the Battle of Lundy's Lane, Leavenworth led a column during a daring night attack on the British lines, and while wounded, he was one of the few senior officers still on his feet after both Generals Brown and Scott

were wounded and removed from the field. He led his regiment on another counterattack that helped push the British off the field. Of the 150 men of the Ninth Infantry at Lundy's Lane, all but 22 were killed or wounded during the battle. After the battle, he received a second brevet, this time to colonel, and returned to his home in Delhi to convalesce with his wife. When the war ended, he resumed his law practice and was elected to the state assembly. Asked to return to the peacetime army after the reductions of 1815, he was appointed major of the Second Infantry and, in 1818, was promoted to lieutenant colonel of the Fifth Infantry. On July 25, 1824, Leavenworth received his brevet promotion to brigadier general, and in 1825, he received command of the Third Infantry, serving as their colonel. He continued to serve on the western frontier, and when the Third arrived at Fort Jesup, he assumed command of the post.[63]

Henry Leavenworth. *Image courtesy of the Frontier Army Museum Fort Leavenworth, KS.*

General Leavenworth immediately realized a major oversight at Fort Jesup: in almost ten years, no one had surveyed the boundary of the military post.

> *I can not* [sic] *discover that any particular reservation of land for military purposes has been made here. The whole country for many miles is public land, except a very few preemption rights, but it is taken up by squatters within a short distance of the Cantonment, that is there are those who reside within less than a mile and one half.*
>
> *There is so much pine timber, that it will require a large trail to supply the garrison with fuel, and it is also, absolutely necessary, to keep those squatters at a respectful distance, for they are the very worst kind of inhabitants, and depend solely upon selling whiskey to our men, by which desertion is continually* [increasing].

The general was also not impressed with the state of repair and design of the buildings at his new command:

> *The buildings here are very inferior, and the men's quarters are too near the officer's quarters.*
>
> *A new Cantont. is necessary, and I hope you will procure an appropriation for that purpose. The Commanding Officer's Quarters consist of a log cabin of two rooms and a hall. It did very well for my predecessor who had no family—at least he was no doubt contented with them. I am not, and request permission to build suitable quarters for the Commanding Officer. It can be done at very small expense. I leave it to you to say how much. It shall be done for whatever [amount] you may allow for the object.[64]*

To protect his supply of useable timber and firewood and to push illegal squatters further away from the post, General Leavenworth issued Order No. 69, Section 5, on November 5, 1831, which allowed:

> *The Assistant Quarter Master will take possession for the United States, for the purpose of supplying fuel to the Garrison, of all public lands lying within three miles of the flag-staff of this Cantonment. He will allow no timber to be cut, or buildings of any kind to be there or erected, except such as may be required for the use of the Government and the troops.*

This expanded the land of the Fort Jesup military reservation to 16,902 acres, covering an area of three square miles, making it one of the largest forts west of the Mississippi. However, the order only applied to those living near the fort who did not have some type of legal claim, creating long-lasting legal problems for the officers of the post.[65]

In January 1832, a new office for the commanding officer was built, and an additional office was added to the guardhouse for the "officer of the guard." Repairs were made to "more or less the whole of the quarters, the kitchens, and other necessary appendages such as store rooms, public stables, etc." Work also began on a block of officers' quarters, which were sixty feet by twenty, built of hewn pine logs and finished around the start of February. Company F departed from Cantonment Atkinson on January 2, 1832, and reached the post on January 15, 1832. Cantonment Atkinson had been a small post on the Calcasieu River founded in 1829 by soldiers from Fort Jesup to prevent smuggling and patrol the southern part of the former Neutral Strip. The post was abandoned in 1832 but would later become the city of Lake Charles, Louisiana. With the arrival of Captain Harrison's company from the Calcasieu, the old commissary stores were "fit up" for quarters for the company. The fort buildings, built a decade earlier, "are fast decaying—the Timbers becoming so rotten as to render some of them dangerous to occupy." The garrison now numbered 249 soldiers.[66]

Since about 1817, there had been a great confusion within the military about the definition of a fort compared to a cantonment, and most new posts opened from the late 1810s through the 1830s were called cantonments. On February 6, 1832, Adjutant General Roger Jones issued General Orders No. 11, which permanently declared "all Military Posts designated Cantonments be hereafter called Forts." Cantonment Jesup received notice of this order in March 1832 and officially changed its name to Fort Jesup.[67]

In March 1834, Leavenworth received word that he had been promoted to command the "Left Wing of the Western Department of the Army," with the responsibility of commanding the southwestern frontier. Leavenworth planned to leave for Fort Gibson on an inspection tour, then to lead an expedition to contact the Plains tribes. He left the post around April 1834 and intended to return to Fort Jesup in September. Lietenant Colonel Vose assumed command of the post on May 19, 1834; the garrison had a strength of 330.[68]

Leavenworth may have planned to return to Fort Jesup in September, but nature had other plans. In August, the garrison received the word that General Leavenworth had died on July 21, 1834, while leading an expedition on the Great Plains. The expedition, which started out with such promise, soon turned into a nightmare. Described as an "ill fated" expedition in the newspapers, it cost the life of 1 general, 2 captains, 1 doctor, 4 lieutenants and 142 enlisted soldiers: 150 officers and men total. Starting out on June 15, 1834, Leavenworth led 8 companies of the Regiment of Dragoons, 27 officers and 500 horsemen, along with 32 Osages, Cherokees, Delawares and Sencas to serve as scouts, interpreters and hunters, as well as a Kiowa and a Pawnee girl to be used as ransom for any white prisoners held by those tribes. Early on, travel was pleasant enough, but soon the summer sun began beating down on the troopers, with temperatures ranging from 103 to 107 degrees, and the rations began running low. It had been hoped that the expedition would be able to live off buffalo hunting, but the dry weather meant that buffalo were not as plentiful as normal. Water was scarce, and when it was found, it was often green with algae, having been contaminated by buffalo herds wallowing in it, trying to stay cool. Diseases such as typhus and dysentery were soon running rampant throughout the column. On the first day, 10 to 12 men dropped out of the march, and by June 26, 1 officer and 27 troopers were left behind at an infantry camp on the Canadian River. Two days later, General Leavenworth fell from his horse while chasing a

Leavenworth's dress uniform coat. *Courtesy of the Frontier Army Museum, Fort Leavenworth, KS.*

buffalo calf. The fall weakened him enough that he became ill with "bilious fever" (most likely a virulent form of cholera), and he died a month later.[69]

On receiving word of the death of their commander, Colonel Vose sent Lieutenants Fry and Barnwell from Fort Towson to the "Fausse Oulchita [*sic*]" to disinter the remains of the late General Leavenworth and Lieutenant McClure. McClure was reinterred at Fort Towson with full military honors, and General Leavenworth's remains left Fort Towson around the eighteenth under the care of Lieutenant Legate and traveled to Natchitoches, where they were met by an escort from Fort Jesup. They then traveled to the post, where "proper honors" were paid them. From Fort Jesup, the procession, now under the charge of Major Belknap, traveled to Delhi, New York, for final interment, which was Leavenworth's wish. Mrs. Leavenworth apparently stayed on post for over a year after her husband's death, as she was listed on an 1835 report as still having quarters at the post. She also made a request to the secretary of war to be appointed post sutler. In December 1834, he wrote to her replying that although the president held her and her late husband in high esteem, he did not feel it was wise to appoint the widows of officers as post sutlers.[70]

With the death of Leavenworth, the War Department promoted James B. Many to the rank of colonel, placed him in command of the Third Infantry on November 21, 1834, and ordered him to assume command of the regimental headquarters at Fort Jesup, transferring him from the Seventh Infantry. Many arrived at the post on January 3, 1835. The garrison housed six companies of the Third Infantry and numbered 268 soldiers.[71]

For more than one thousand years, the Caddo had been the primary Native American culture in northwest Louisiana. Made up of a series of tribal bands, each with a unique but interconnected language, trade and religion, the Caddo were a powerful society when the French and Spanish arrived in the early eighteenth century. However, by the 1830s, a combination of factors such as disease; shifting weather patterns, which varied yearly from

Harriet Lovejoy Leavenworth. *Image courtesy of the Frontier Army Museum Fort Leavenworth, KS.*

drought conditions to widespread flooding; a decrease in the availability of wild game; intertribal raiding; and an increase in the number of white settlers in the region would all lead to the near depopulation of the tribe. In March 1835, Indian agent Jehiel Brooks received word from the government to begin negotiating with the Caddo to sell their lands in Louisiana. Under economic pressure, desiring to maintain some level of cultural and tribal

This page: Park volunteers wearing reproductions of 1832 uniforms. *Photos by Dennis Self, author's collection.*

sovereignty and fearing that they might be forcefully removed if they did not negotiate, the Caddo agreed to listen to the proposal.[72]

On June 16, 1835, Brooks sent a request to Colonel Many that troops from Fort Jesup be sent to the treaty ground. Many sent Company F, Third U.S. Infantry, under the command of Captain T. J. Harrison, which left the fort on June 21, 1835, for the Caddo Agency on the Red River. The force, which consisted of two lieutenants, an acting surgeon and about fifty soldiers, arrived at the agency house around four o'clock in the afternoon on June 27. These soldiers were not sent to threaten the Caddo into signing the treaty (in fact, they would have been outnumbered almost five to one); instead, the soldiers were there to protect the proceedings from being disrupted by a small but vocal element of Caddo unhappy with the treaty or by several former Spanish subjects living around Bayou Pierre, such as Manual Flores, who hated anything American and who was trying to prevent the treaty. In fact, Flores and several others, including Francis Bark and Joseph Valentin, were stopped by the soldiers and forced to leave before they could make trouble. One member of the command was Joseph Bonnell, an 1825 graduate of West Point, who attempted to read the English version of the treaty before it was signed. He was prevented from reading the copy by Brooks, and later, Bonnell discovered that Brooks had written a clause into the treaty that allowed him to purchase large tracts of prime land for a fraction of the cost. Bonnell reported the incident, and in 1850, it reached the U.S. Supreme Court.[73]

After much discussion within the tribe, the Caddo agreed to sell their lands in northwest Louisiana, an area roughly between five hundred thousand and one million acres, for $30,000 worth of horses and trade goods, plus cash payments of $10,000 for the next five years totaling $80,000 (roughly $2,555,891 in 2022). This land, modern-day Caddo and part of DeSoto Parish, was prime river bottom land, well suited for growing vegetables and cash crops such as cotton. It quickly attracted settlers. Shreve Town (later known as Shreveport) would grow into the third-largest city in Louisiana and has become a major industrial, educational and cultural center of North Louisiana. Fort Jesup's role in helping to open and clear the Red River in the 1820s and early 1830s, before the arrival of Captain Henry Miller Shreve in 1833, and its role in allowing the orderly negotiation of the treaty between the Caddo and the United States helped set the stage for the founding of Shreveport. Although some Caddo remained in Louisiana, most moved first into Texas within a year of the treaty but were soon displaced and eventually moved to the region around Binger, Oklahoma. Jeff Girard, retired regional

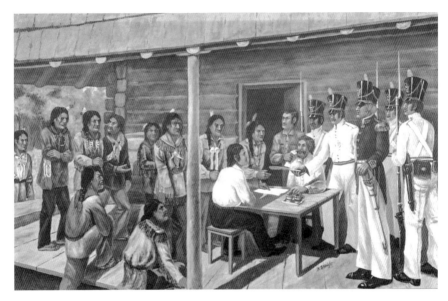

Signing of the Treaty with the Caddo Nation. Courtesy of the Louisiana State Exhibit Museum, Shreveport. Brian Lewis, photographer.

archaeologist, paid a fitting tribute to the Caddo at the end of his book on Caddo archeology: "Caddo culture is a fundamental component of the heritage of the state of Louisiana. It is truly unfortunate that the legacy of the Caddo people, a legacy that comprises the major portion of the human past in the northwest portion of the state, is so poorly known and rarely appreciated and celebrated."[74]

The winter of 1835–36 would see a rapid shift from the peacetime army routine on the frontier, as the small U.S. Army began preparing to fight two wars on two fronts separated by one thousand miles. On December 28, the Seminole Indians in Florida went on the warpath, ambushing and massacring a detachment of 108 soldiers under the command of Major Francis Dade, and at roughly the same time, the resentment between settlers in Texas and Mexico over the abolishing of the Mexican Constitution of 1824 led to open revolt. The Texas Revolution would have the most immediate impact on the garrison of Fort Jesup, while the Second Seminole War would have the most long reaching.

CHAPTER 5

FORT JESUP AND THE TEXAS REVOLUTION

From the time of the Louisiana Purchase, many Americans had their eyes on the vast open expanses of Texas, which were either underpopulated or not settled at all. At a time when land was becoming more expensive and harder to get in the United States, the fertile fields of Texas looked like the promised land. Of course, there was the double problem that the land was owned by a foreign government and that much of the best farmland lay in the traditional territory of Native American tribes that were not friendly to settlers. However, these were seen as only minor difficulties, and some of the more enterprising settlers had a solution. They would help Texas shake off the "yoke of tyranny" and then help it become part of the United States of America. Fort Jesup, as America's closest military post to Texas, would have a front-row seat, and the actions and inactions of her officers and men would have a lasting effect on American history.

During the 1820s, one of Fort Jesup's missions was to monitor events in Texas and Mexico and, after American immigration to Mexico was legalized in April 1823, protecting the waves of settlers traveling by road to Texas. However, by the end of the decade, relations between Mexico and her northern province began to sour. Several factors on both sides led to growing hostility. Growing nationalism in Mexico led to jealousy of the prosperity of the Americans in Texas, who were not only growing in number and wealth but who also, by agreements dating from the early 1820s, paid almost no taxes or duties. Texas, on the other hand, was pushing for statehood within the Mexican Republic. Although, during much of the Spanish era, Texas was considered a province of New Spain. However, by the end of the Mexican Revolution, the population had been so depleted that when Mexico created its new republic, Texas was combined with the state of Coahuila. Texas felt that with its growing population, it deserved to be a separate state, with representation in the Mexican congress. Mexico saw this statehood movement as one more attempt by Americans to separate Texas from Mexico. The growing distrust of the Americans in Texas would lead to a ban on immigration from the United States to Mexico, meaning that all the settlers now traveling down the Texas Road through Fort Jesup would be crossing into Mexico illegally.[75]

All settlers came to Texas to start a new life, but some had more than just an economic need to start over. For some, their businesses had failed, or their debts were higher than they could pay, and for others, there was some type of personal issue or rumor that brought shame to their reputation. All over the United States, men would write the letters "GTT" on their cabins, letting family, friends, neighbors, creditors and lawyers know that they had "gone to Texas" and that they were out of reach of all legal issues they may have been dealing with once they crossed the Sabine. One citizen of Rapides Parish described the so-called GTTs in this way: "Whenever an individual becomes somewhat embarrassed, he crosses the Sabine with all his property and remains in perfect security."[76] Many of these GTTs crossed through Fort Jesup on their way to their new home, and while most were not famous when they went to Texas, many would shape Texas and American history.[77]

One traveler who already had a reputation was Jim Bowie, who traveled through Fort Jesup on his way to Texas in 1826. He was on the verge of making a small fortune on forged land documents in Louisiana and Arkansas when he heard of the 1825 change in Mexican land policy, which allowed for more *empizros* (American land investors who were given land in exchange for bringing settlers into Texas) and settlers not attached to the current *empizro* program, opening even more land for settlement. It was an opportunity that Bowie could not pass up. He left Alexandria, where he was living, for Natchez, Mississippi, to conduct business and then traveled first by steamboat in late May or early June for Natchitoches, then by horse down the Texas Road through Fort Jesup to Gaines's Ferry, where he crossed the Sabine River into Texas. While this was not his final trip to Texas, it was the trip where he began laying the groundwork for his future land deals by announcing his intention to become a Mexican citizen and swearing his intent to convert to Catholicism. It was also the trip where he met his future wife, Maria Ursula, the daughter of the Juan Martin de Veramendi San Antonio's alcalde and most influential citizen.[78]

Another future Alamo leader who would have barely attracted notice when he made his trek to Texas through Fort Jesup was William Travis. By 1831, Travis's financial and personal issues were almost unsurmountable. While he was a somewhat successful lawyer with modest but irregular fees, he was also running a newspaper that did not have the circulation or the advertising it needed to support itself, so what little money Travis was making as a lawyer was being used to cover the debts the newspaper was incurring. Although the details were never revealed, it was known that Travis's marriage was not a happy one. As was common practice in the early nineteenth century, both Travis and his wife, Rosanna, were young when they married (Travis was nineteen, and Rosanna was sixteen), but as they grew older, they also grew apart. Their first son was born not long after their marriage, and soon, another child was on the way. It was never proven, but according to small-town gossip, this child was not Travis's. The final straw was in March 1831, when Travis was charged with failure to pay his debts by multiple creditors. Unable to pay and unwilling to go to debtors' prison, Travis readied his horse for the long journey to the Sabine. He traveled from his home in Claiborne, Alabama, to Natchez, Mississippi, where he crossed into Louisiana and traveled to Alexandria, turning north toward Natchitoches, then west down the Texas Road through Fort Jesup, entering Texas in late April or early May and arriving at Austin's headquarters town of San Felipe during the first week of May.[79]

After the Fredonian Rebellion, Mexico City decided to send troops to Nacogdoches and other key points in Texas. Colonel Jose de las Piedras was sent to Nacogdoches with a force of 160 infantry and 60 mounted dragoons. While this seemed to be a strong force, Piedras was concerned that if trouble broke out, the armed settlers between Nacogdoches and the Sabine combined with the garrison at Fort Jesup could number as many as three thousand within only a few days. He also had supply issues, often having to depend on the merchants in Natchitoches to supply his troops with ammunition, clothing and other supplies. On one of his many supply trips to Natchitoches, the colonel and four of his staff officers were honored with a ball at Fort Jesup that began on February 22, 1832. It was described as a "most splendid Ball" and lasted for three days and nights.[80]

Another officer of the Mexican Army who was entertained at Fort Jesup was Juan Nepomuceno Almonte, who had been sent on a secret military and political inspection tour of Texas. As part of his 1834 inspection of Texas, Colonel Juan Almonte traveled through Louisiana to try to determine the feelings of Americans toward Texas and to find out if the American government was massing troops on the border for an invasion. He left New Orleans sometime after March 19, 1834, and arrived in Natchitoches on April 2. Both community leaders and military officers, including Leavenworth, assumed that Almonte was part of the Mexican Boundary Commission; the colonel allowed them to believe it and reported what they told him to the Mexican State Department. Without realizing it, Leavenworth eased many of Almonte's fears about President Jackson amassing a large strike force on the border by inviting the colonel to be his guest at Fort Jesup. In a historical twist of fate, it was Almonte's visit to Fort Jesup that led him to recommend a smaller number of troops be sent to Texas then he had originally planned to suggest. Had Mexico sent a larger army into the province, it is likely that the revolution would have been crushed before it began.[81]

A series of events would lead to the separation of Texas from Mexico. Only a few Texans took notice when Antonio Lopez de Santa Anna was elected president of Mexico in 1833, and most who did were happy with his election because he had run on a platform of reform and increased states' rights. However, within a year, all that had changed. To consolidate his own power, he disbanded the congress and abolished the Constitution of 1824. While there were major differences between the U.S. constitution and the Mexican constitution, there were enough similarities that the settlers had felt comfortable living under the Mexican constitution. Santa Anna's power grab represented not only financial ruin for most of the settlers but also the loss of the freedoms they had enjoyed for over ten years. Even as late as the fall of 1835, there was still a larger number of settlers pushing for peace than for war, but that would soon change.

Open warfare between the Texas colonists and Mexico began on October 2, 1835, when a detachment of Mexican cavalry attempted to remove the small canon given by the Mexican government to the town of Gonzales. Under a homemade flag with "Come and Take It!" written on it, the townspeople fired the canon and their rifles into the advancing Mexicans, killing one soldier and plunging the people of Texas into war.[82]

Once conflict broke out between the Texans and Mexican forces, the Texas assembly began to organize an army. Sam Houston was selected to command the regular army of the new republic but was not placed in command of the volunteers or given command of the entire army at this time. One of his difficulties lay in trying to recruit men for the regular army's longer term of enlistment—as compared to the shorter terms for volunteer and militia units—and finding men who were willing to be held to a higher level of discipline (including not being able to elect their own officers, like the volunteer units could), even though they were given more land and larger enlistment bonuses. Providing uniforms, supplies and weapons would be another problem facing the Texas government. A simple solution was to recruit officers with military experience and troops already used to stricter discipline and equipped with their own uniforms, weapons and equipment. The easiest place to find these men was Fort Jesup, and efforts were made to bring these troops into the war on the side of Texas. As word spread about the land bonuses being offered, more and more soldiers and even a few officers began slipping away from Fort Jesup to join the Texas army. Many enlistees in the Texas army were former soldiers from Fort Jesup who had either gone to Texas after their term of service was completed or had deserted before 1835 and gone to Texas to start a new life.[83]

One of the officers who was heavily recruited for the Texas cause was Lieutenant Joseph Bonnell, who had earlier distinguished himself during the Caddo Treaty negotiations in July 1835. On November 22, 1835, the General Council of Texas and the governor of Texas approved Sam Houston's request to name Bonnell as his aid-de-camp with a commission of captain in the Texas regular army. Bonnell requested a leave of absence from the U.S. Army to take the aid-de-camp position, but the War Department would not grant him leave, stating that it would be a violation of U.S. neutrality for an active U.S. officer to serve with the revolutionary army fighting against Mexico. Unwilling to just desert like some other officers had, and due to the ill health of his wife, Bonnell wrote Houston to inform him that he could not take the position offered. Bonnell did include in his letter a list of instructions on how to inventory equipment, issue army supplies and organize the companies; he also provided several manuals.

Bonnell may not have been able to join the Texas army, but the Texas army never revoked his commission, leaving his name on the roll of active duty officers of the army. This gives Bonnell the honor of being the only officer in Texas history to hold a commission with two governments at the same time.[84]

The fall and early winter of 1835–36 had seen a series of Texas victories; in fact, many people in both Texas and the United States thought the war was over. But the next three months would not only prove that the war was not over but would also cost the lives of hundreds of Texas soldiers, including several former Fort Jesup soldiers. Most in the Texas government and army felt that Santa Anna would either not advance on Texas or, if he did, it would take months for him to assemble an army and march from Mexico to Texas. It was assumed that late March or early April would be the earliest that the Mexicans would reach Texas, because no one thought that Santa Anna would risk marching his army through the mountains of northern Mexico in the winter. The Texans were caught completely off guard when, on February 23, Santa Anna marched into San Antonio, almost a month earlier than expected. Soldiers, settlers, women and children fled into the Alamo, which the Mexicans soon surrounded, starting a thirteen-day siege. For the next two weeks, there was a consistent artillery barrage, and a series of probing attacks were launched to find weakness in the fortifications. At five o'clock in the morning on March 6, Santa Anna launched his attack. Over one thousand Mexican soldiers stormed over the walls, killing all the defenders, including William Travis, Jim Bowie, David Crockett and at least three former Fort Jesup soldiers (William Fishbaugh, Company B; William Johnson, Company A; and Edward Nelson, Company I). Another group of Alamo defenders who were killed were members of the New Orleans Greys, who had been recruited in New Orleans and outfitted in uniforms that were either surplus 1821 military uniforms or so close that they were often mistaken for regular troops. One company took the sea route to Texas, while one traveled to Texas through Natchitoches. Unsure how they would be received by the garrison at Fort Jesup, which was supposed to maintain neutrality and stop any armed groups moving into Texas, the Greys left the Texas Road and traveled through the woods to bypass the fort. Less than a month after the fall of the Alamo, Fannin's command at Goliad was defeated and surrendered. On Palm Sunday (March 21), the unarmed survivors were marched out of the fort and massacred, while those in the hospital were shot in their beds.[85]

Hearing of the Mexican pledge of "no quarter" and seeing the proof after the fall of the Alamo and Fannin's defeat at Goliad, thousands of civilian settlers began fleeing their homes and heading for the safety of the United States. As one eyewitness recorded:

> *Hundreds of families were returning from Texas, and there was more misery among them than could well be imagined. All throughout the woods, were living under sheds, those going to Texas, who had been stopped by the accounts they had heard, and others who were returning to their old homes. Under the same sheds were to be seen blacks and whites, who had sickened with measles, some of whom were constantly dying, and the whole destitute of the means of relief. It made one's heart sick to witness these spectacles.*[86]

The frontier was in a total state of confusion when General Gaines arrived in Natchitoches on April 4, and on the eighth, he sent letters to the governors of Louisiana, Mississippi, Alabama and Tennessee, informing them of Secretary of War Cass's January 23 instructions to remain neutral, reminding them of the government's obligation under the Treaty of 1831 to prevent tribes from crossing into Texas and asking for volunteers from the states, urging that most of them be mounted. Gaines also wrote to the secretary of state, informing him that he had learned that many Indians had crossed into Texas from the United States and that Santa Anna was rapidly advancing, leaving a path of destruction behind him. Gaines wrote that he believed that when the Mexicans reached the Trinity River, this would be the signal for the tribes to go on the warpath through Texas. Gaines's goal was to have a large enough force of regulars and volunteers to calm the fears of the settlers and to "inflict summary punishment on such of the enemy by whom they are now menaced as may teach them to respect us, and in future to pay more regard than they seem now disposed to pay to our rights and treaties."[87]

After receiving numerous reports of Mexican agents among the tribes and of large numbers of warriors advancing on the frontier settlements, Gaines ordered his command to march to the Sabine River and to set up camp near the site of General Wilkinson's 1806 camp. Most of the garrison left for the Sabine River on April 13, 1836, with additional companies leaving Fort Jesup for the Sabine River on April 18, leaving Brevet Major B. Riley, Sixth Infantry, in command of the post, with ninety-seven soldiers. General Gaines ordered the post quartermaster to purchase mules and horses to furnish transportation for the supplies and for the nine companies of the Sixth Infantry and five companies of the Third Infantry.

It would have been possible for Gaines to cross the river in force to "investigate" the Indian rumors, and on the march, he encountered several hundred women and children along with some male settlers who begged him to do just that, but instead of rushing headlong into an international situation, he ordered his men to set up a long-term camp on the American side of the Sabine River and gave it the name Camp Sabine. Before leaving for the Sabine River, General Gaines had sent Joseph Bonnell to the Caddo villages to determine if they were planning to go on the warpath. Bonnell reported to Gaines at Camp Sabine on April 20 that he had arrived at the Caddo villages on April 14 and learned that Manuel Flores had been among the Caddo about two months earlier, promising the Caddo plunder if they would help destroy the Texans, whom he represented as mainly Americans. Flores had also told the Caddo that the Americans were marching toward

Reproduction army tents like those that would have been used in 1836. *Photo by author.*

Park volunteers portraying a scene at a military camp in 1836. *Photo by Dennis Self, author's collection.*

their villages to kill them. Bonnell found that the villages were deserted of warriors, normally a sign that they were on the warpath, but he learned that the warriors had actually left the villages to avoid trouble with the Anglos. Bonnell learned that while the Caddo did not intend to join Flores in attacks on the Anglos, they did believe that the Texans intended to attack them, which was why they had not returned to their villages to plant corn. The information calmed some of the fears that the Caddo would join the fight, but the fact the Flores was still with the warriors on the plains and the fears of the settlers on both sides of the Sabine River that the Cherokees or some of the Plains tribes, such as the Comanches, might begin raiding led General Gaines to maintain his request for mounted troops to be at Camp Sabine as soon as possible after May 1.[88]

Bonnell's mission was a critical but often overlooked aspect of the Texas Revolution. An important aspect of the Texas Revolution was the threat from Native American groups. As rumors grew of Mexican agents trying to stir up the tribes, many in the Texas government were pushing Houston to split his already small army to protect settlements and many of his soldiers were deserting to return home to protect their families. Bonnell's agreement with the Caddo that they would not join with the Mexican forces not only allowed Houston to hold his small army together but also may have even prevented a surprise attack on Houston's army as it marched from the Brazos River to San Jacinto, as was being suggested by some of the warriors. Not only was this critical to the outcome of the war, but Bonnell's mission was also very dangerous, as he was traveling with only himself and a few soldiers in a foreign country at war. Had he been captured by a Mexican patrol, he probably would have been executed as a spy; if a rogue band of Indians attacked his group, they would have been outnumbered and killed. If the Caddo had truly been on the warpath, or if they had been allied with another tribe on the warpath, there is a good chance the group would have been either killed or turned over to the Mexicans. For his bravery and the importance of his mission, the Texas legislature in 2005 passed a resolution declaring Bonnell a "hero of the Texas Revolution" and placing a historical marker at his grave site.[89]

In April, it appeared the colonists might finally get a lucky break. Houston had been heading toward East Texas trying to gather men and supplies while training his army as best as possible and staying ahead of Santa Anna's army. Sam Houston would maintain that his plan had always been to draw Santa Anna into a situation favorable for the Texans, but a look at the map shows that Houston was in fact drawing Santa Anna closer and closer to the Sabine

River and the U.S. Army. While he had no way of knowing what Gaines would do if the Mexican Army approached American territory, Houston probably assumed that they would be supportive of the Texans. However, many of Houston's political enemies in both the government and the army were claiming that Houston's withdrawal was a sign of cowardice. Houston was losing more men from desertion then he was gaining, and he knew if he did not do something soon, there would not be an army left. It was at this critical juncture that Houston received word that Santa Anna had split his army, and while the odds were not even, they were now at least closer. When Santa Anna set up camp in a swamp with limited escape routes, Houston knew he had to attack before the two parts of the Mexican Army reunited. On April 21, the Texas army attacked Santa Anna's forces at San Jacinto.[90]

Sam Houston's army was an unmilitary sight as they followed their general, himself dressed in a "shirt that had once been white, a vest, a shabby black coat, mud-spattered yellowish-brown trousers, and warn-out [sic] boots." The troops wore a mixture of clothing, everything from buckskin to wool frocks and tailcoats, with a smattering of U.S. Army uniforms. The equipment the soldiers carried varied as much as the clothing they wore. Their shoulder arms were a combination of hunting rifles, "surplus" military muskets, bowie knifes, tomahawks and bayonets. The artillery company was made up of two iron six-pound cannons, pulled by twenty soldiers each because the oxen had been reclaimed by their owner.[91]

Earlier that morning, Santa Anna had decided that the Texans would not launch an attack, and he and most of his troops were taking an afternoon siesta. Once the Texans were noticed, the Mexicans fired a nine-pound cannon, whose shot went high over the heads of the advancing Texans. Sam Houston ordered the men to advance faster but to hold their fire until they got closer. He next ordered the cannons to open fire. The first shots hit the Mexican breastworks and quickly began silencing the Mexican cannons with highly effective counterbattery. The effectiveness of this fire was surprising, since the Texas Army had not had the time nor the extra powder and shot for intensive artillery training, but they were blessed with several soldiers familiar with artillery tactics—tactics learned on the parade ground at Fort Jesup. Because Fort Jesup had never been garrisoned by artillery units, the infantrymen had been trained in firing cannons. This opening phase of the battle, which helped lay the groundwork for the Texas victory, was in the hands of several former Fort Jesup soldiers. In January, Privates Michael Campbell, George Cumberland, J.N. Gainer and Ira Milliman had been transferred from Henry Teal's company of Texas Rangers to the regular artillery company, and all were listed as deserters from the Third Infantry, Companies B, E, F and H, respectively. Four other men had been transferred from Captain Amasa Turner's company of regulars, including Ellis Benson, who was discharged from the Third in February 1834. The three other men were Joseph A Clayton, Joseph Merwin and Seneca Legg. These men were now laying down effective artillery fire, allowing the Texas Army to advance.[92]

The center position of the Texas line was held by Lieutenant Colonel Henry Millard's regular company, which consisted of many U.S. deserters from Fort Jesup and was armed with faster-loading smoothbore muskets, which, unlike a rifle, could be fitted with a bayonet. One of the regulars, William C. Swearingen, wrote to his brother in Kentucky after the battle that "riflemen opened fire at 100 yards and the 'musketry' advanced farther before they fired….We were ordered to charge with our bayonets," and then "the enemy gave way except about sixty men around the cannon. They were protected by a breastwork of corn sacks, salt, barrels of meat and boxes of canister shot. They fell by the bayonet and swam in one mangle heap from that time until they reached the bieau [bayou]."[93]

Sam Houston downplayed any U.S. involvement for political and diplomatic reasons and claimed that there were no bayonets in the Texas Army, instead claiming that all hand-to-hand combat was done with the butts of the Texans' rifles. One modern historian, Dr. Terrence Barragy, believes that "the bayonets and the Regulars' fast, accurate fire, along with the artillery handled by experienced soldiers, may have contributed to the early panic in the Mexican army," laying the groundwork for the Texas victory."[94]

The exact number of U. S. troops involved in the Texas Revolution and the number of those from Fort Jesup may never be known, and certainly, the number will continue to be debated. Some historians have placed the number at over two hundred, and some claim that there were no U.S.

U.S. bayonet, pattern 1816. *Photo by author.*

soldiers involved. Several factors have added to the confusion: many of the names in both the Texas Army and the U.S. Army are common names, such as Smith, Jones, Brown and Johnson; many of the soldiers joining the Texas Army used only initials or changed their names; and the company clerks did not help the situation by often spelling names phonetically, rather than asking how they were spelled. Some of these deserters would remain in Texas, apply for land grants and become part of Texas society, with some even becoming elected officials, while others would return to Fort Jesup and be reinstated with no court-martial.[95]

Santa Anna's defeat would lead to Texas's independence, and while the role of Fort Jesup and other U.S. troops in the victory was downplayed for political reasons by both the Texas and the U.S. governments, the fort's strategic location and the number of highly trained regular soldiers from the fort who fought in the war would play a key role in the founding of the Republic of Texas. Many of the soldiers from Fort Jesup would help create Texas society by founding communities, protecting Texas as members of the Texas Army or Texas Rangers, starting businesses or holding political office. However, it would be over ten years before Mexico would honor Texas's claim of independence, and the U.S. army still had a war to fight in Florida.

CHAPTER 6

"WARS, AND THE RUMOR OF WARS"

etween the spring of 1836 and the spring of 1844, Fort Jesup
settled back into a routine of frontier garrison duties; however,
local and national events would affect the course of history for
the troops on the Louisiana border. Even after the Texas victory at the
Battle of San Jacinto, Fort Jesup remained a busy place. Troops were kept
on the Sabine River to guard the border, and the army was engaged in
combat operations in Florida against the Seminoles, a conflict that would
become the longest Indian War in American history, lasting almost eight
years. The United States was still unsure how to react to the new country
on its western boundary, and Mexico was not only refusing to recognize
its breakaway republic but was also threatening to reinvade Texas and, if
necessary, march its armies to Washington, D.C. Also creating tension were
the growing abolitionist movement and the increasing sectional differences
that were threatening, even in the 1830s, to tear the country apart. When
Doctor Nathan Jarvis wrote in an 1837 letter that "we receive…[reports
of] wars, and rumors of wars," he very accurately described the uneasiness
and uncertainty of the era.

While most of the nation's attention was on the fighting in Texas, the
United States began its longest and bloodiest Indian war. The Second
Seminole War began on December 28, 1835, when a detachment of
infantrymen and artillerymen, under the command of Brevet Major
Francis L. Dade, was ambushed and massacred on the road between Fort
King and Fort Brooke. Fighting in the swamps of Florida would last for
the next eight years, and while it would not directly affect Fort Jesup for the

first couple of months, as the war progressed, it would strip all the western forts of men and resources.[96]

To monitor the situation in Texas, General Gaines maintained his headquarters at Camp Sabine until September 1836. Major Nelson was in command of Fort Jesup in September 1836, with 91 men. October 1836 saw the return of Companies D and K of the Third Infantry to Fort Jesup from Camp Sabine, as well as Companies A, B, F, G and H of the Sixth Infantry, all of whom arrived on October 9. This brought the garrison up to 366 soldiers, with Major Thompson in command. Major Nelson assumed command of the post in December 1836. The garrison was reduced to 112 soldiers with the transfer of Company H, Third Infantry, to Camp Worth, and orders were received for the Sixth Infantry to move to Florida. Two to four companies of infantry would be stationed at Camp Sabine until the summer of 1838. With the end of combat operations in the Texas Revolution, the steady stream of settlers and travelers soon returned to the Texas Road in ever-increasing numbers, and Fort Jesup returned to its role of frontier guardian, protecting the settlers as they moved to their new homes in the Republic of Texas.[97]

Once it was clear that a war over Texas would not be fought, the War Department began redirecting resources from the Sabine. All new recruits who joined the army were sent to Florida until May 1837, as well as all new uniforms and equipment. The first troops to be deployed from Fort Jesup to Florida were elements of the Sixth Infantry, who received transfer orders in December 1836, but they would not be the last.[98]

Colonel Many resumed command of the post on January 3, 1837, at the end of his furlough. Companies C, D and E of the Sixth Infantry arrived at Fort Jesup on January 23 from New Orleans and left the next day for the Sabine River to relieve Company B, Third Infantry, which arrived back at Jesup on January 18, and Company H, Third Infantry, returned from Camp Worth on January 31, 1837, bringing the troop strength to 191. The garrison almost doubled in size in May 1837, when the adjutant general ordered that new recruits be sent to Forts Jesup, Gibson and Leavenworth instead of the war zone in Florida. When the detachment of 177 soldiers arrived, it brought the strength of the post to 357 total men.[99]

In 1837, Brevet Major Belknap was given instructions to begin clearing the Sabine River for navigation. He was placed in command of two companies of the Third Infantry and given authorization to select a position near the mouth of the Sabine to establish a supply depot. Because he was in command of two companies, he was given major's pay and double rations, and his men were given extra-duty pay while on this assignment. To clear the river, the quartermaster issued Belknap an assortment of tools and items, everything from fifty felling axes, carpenter's tools, a two-horse wagon, two reams of writing paper and one hundred quills. Major Belknap left the fort on July 10 with 113 men and arrived at Camp Sabine on the twelfth to begin work on clearing the river. Their work led to even more economic growth and the founding of dozens of river ports on both sides of the Sabine.

With the end of the Texas Revolution, and the financial panic of 1837, Fort Jesup's existence was placed in danger as the War Department discussed closing the fort and moving the garrison closer to the Sabine River. Colonel Many defended the fort's location by arguing that "you can always have an efficient force at it…ready to move in any direction" and that the fort was centrally located to defend most of the settlements in west-central Louisiana. Congress had appropriated $25,000 dollars for "the erection of Barracks, Quarters, Store Houses, Hospital, and Stables," but work was never started because of the Texas Revolution and the uncertainty over whether the garrison would remain at Fort Jesup, move to the Sabine River or even move into Texas. When the dust settled in Texas, in June 1837, the quartermaster's department requested funds to repair and expand the fort. Secretary of War John R. Poinsett felt that the fort was "too remote from the frontier and ought to be abandoned," but after communicating with Colonel Many, he felt that if nothing else, the post should "be retained for place of refuge in case of sickness among the troops on the Sabine." Work began on November 2, 1837, and the fort was not only saved from abandonment but would also be rebuilt and enlarged.[100]

On November 22, 1837, Fort Jesup's new doctor arrived on post. Dr. John Emerson was born in Pennsylvania sometime around 1803 and earned his medical degree from the University of Pennsylvania in 1824. He practiced medicine for several years and served as a civilian contract surgeon at Jefferson Barracks, passed the Army Medical Review Board in October 1833 and received an appointment as an assistant surgeon on October 25, 1833, to take effect on December 1 of the same year. Emerson seems to have been a skilled doctor, earning the respect of General Atkinson for his term as a contract surgeon and a commendation from the general for the "manor in which the duty has been performed by him, since he has been employed in the public services." The doctor was stationed at Forts Armstrong and Snelling before he was ordered to Fort Jesup. While at Fort Snelling, Emerson began requesting a transfer to a more southern post, claiming that the harsh weather in the North was contributing to his ill health. He had hoped to be

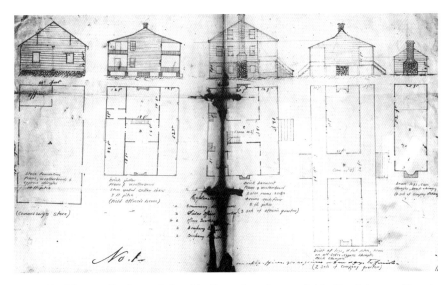

Plan of buildings at Fort Jesup. *Left to right*: Commissary's store, field officer's house, officers' quarters, company quarters, company kitchens. *Courtesy of the Louisiana Office of State Parks, Fort Jesup State Historic Site.*

transferred back to Jefferson Barracks, having spent most of his adult life in St. Louis, and he got his wish when on October 20, 1837, he received transfer orders to St. Louis—but unfortunately for the good doctor, Emerson had only been in St. Louis a short time when transfer orders reached him ordering him to proceed to Fort Jesup. Unhappy with the transfer, Emerson had barely arrived at Fort Jesup before his complaints to the surgeon general (who had served at Fort Jesup in the 1820s) began. In letter after letter to the surgeon general, Dr. Emerson complained about the weather, his health and his distance from his land and his colleagues.

However, life at Fort Jesup was not all bad for Dr. Emerson, because in February 1838, he met Eliza Irene Sanford of St. Louis. She was at the post visiting her sister, Mary Bainbridge, the wife of Captain Henry Bainbridge. On February 6, 1838, Dr. Emerson and Irene were married in Natchitoches. Shortly after his marriage, Doctor Emerson sent for his slaves, Dred Scott and his wife, Harriet Scott (the two had been married in a civil ceremony, which was very uncommon at the time). Emerson had purchased Dred Scott sometime before December 1, 1833, from the Blow family in St. Louis, and while Scott rarely traveled with the doctor to a new post, it was common for Emerson to send for him after he was established at his new station. Dred Scott lived at Fort Jesup from April 1838 until September 1838, when Dr. Emerson received a transfer back to Fort Snelling.[101]

Because of Fort Jesup's location in the South, the officers and soldiers stationed there were sure to find themselves in the middle of the increasing controversy over slavery. The issue of slavery had been with the garrison since the beginning of the post; in fact, the post's location near the large plantations along the Red River was not an accident. In the event of a slave revolt, the regular soldiers were to provide support to local law enforcement and militia. The fact that many of the officers were from states where slavery was outlawed and many had mixed feelings about slavery did not enter into the military's plans. After the Nat Turner uprising in 1831, Secretary of War Lewis Cass issued orders to Fort Jesup that "in case of any application from the authorities or citizens of Alexandria…[they were] to detach an adequate force for that place, to preserve order, if…circumstances should justify it."

Just such an "application" would happen in the fall of 1837, when the garrison received an emergency request from the Rapides Committee of Vigilance for two companies to be sent to the region to help put down a slave revolt. The revolt was exposed by Lewis Chaney, the slave of David Cheney, in early October, and he claimed the revolt was "better planned and managed than any before." The plot involved a few whites, several

Hospital site at Fort Jesup. Dred Scott would have walked these grounds while at Fort Jesup. *Photo by author.*

free people of color and nearly fifty slaves on six plantations along Bayou Rapides and Bayou Boeuf. Coming on the heels of a plot two years earlier, it was taken seriously by the citizens of the region. The catch was, Lewis Chaney was not only a stool pigeon, but he was also the leader of the revolt. According to Solomon Northup, another slave in the area, Chaney's original plan had been to take his group of refugee slaves to Mexico, which had abolished slavery in 1829; he hoped that Mexican nationals still living in the Republic of Texas would help his group reach Mexico. Under the cover of darkness, he traveled from plantation to plantation recruiting members and gathering supplies. Northup described Lewis Chaney as "an avenging angel, more intelligent than the generality of his race," as well as "shrewd, cunning…unscrupulous and full of treachery." He gained the support of other slaves by telling them how he hated his master for removing him from the relative comfort of a position as house servant and making him a field hand. He timed the plot to coincide with the annual fever season, when most of the white residents would leave the area for healthier locations. He played on the growing abolition movement to gain support from white residents, and he also had the help of an unidentified Spaniard. Apparently, the plot did not include mass murder—until his plan was blown.

When his cache of supplies was discovered in a swamp behind the Hawkins plantation, Chaney changed his plans, and the changes did not involve loyalty to his fellow conspiracy members. To save his own neck, Lewis Chaney informed his master that he had learned of a slave plot that would involve the massacre of the plantation owners and their families. Lewis's master, David, quickly called a meeting at the parish courthouse on October 6 to organize patrols and call for help from Fort Jesup. Before the federal troops arrived, bands of armed citizens began to arrest and execute alleged conspiracy members.

Companies D and K of the Third Infantry (about one hundred soldiers) marched from Fort Jesup; they arrived four days later, on October 10, and quicky restored order, although not in the way that the residents of Alexandria expected. The soldiers destroyed the gallows that had been used to execute nine slaves and three free people of color. They freed most of the prisoners, although thirty slave conspirators remained in confinement to await a legal trial. During the sixteen days that the soldiers were in the field, one soldier died in a drowning accident, and eight soldiers deserted. Of the eight deserters, three were soon captured and sent back to Fort Jesup for court-martial. The three deserters were found guilty and sentenced to receive fifty lashes and hard labor with a ball and chain. The soldiers from

Fort Jesup were requested to protect the plantation owners from their slaves, but in the end, they did more to protect the slaves from their masters and from mob justice. They were able to end vigilante justice and prevent mob rule during the uprising, saving the lives of even more enslaved persons. In the end, Lewis Cheney earned his freedom and was even given $500 to cover his expenses to leave the state by the Louisiana legislature, but his freedom cost the lives of many of his coconspirators. His role as leader of the revolt was not discovered by the authorities until he was already out of the state.[102]

In May 1838, E.B. Alexander oversaw the closing of Camp Sabine, after the three companies of the Sixth Infantry left for Florida. The extra horses and oxen that were not needed for the use of Fort Jesup were sold; the clothing that had arrived for the detachment of the Sixth was sent to the headquarters of the regiment at Tampa Bay, Florida; all of the useable public property "worth saving" was sent to Fort Jesup; and a "worthy person" was placed in charge of the buildings until the War Department decided what to do with the camp. Eventually, it would become a house of worship, and the site is still used by Beulah Baptist Church.[103]

A report arrived to Colonel Many from "highly respectable citizens" on November 29, 1838, informing him that about 160 men of the Army of the Republic of Texas, under the command of General Rusk, had crossed the Red River to attack groups of Caddo who had remained in the United States. A letter in the *Army and Navy Chronicle*, written by one of the officers from Fort Jesup, informed the readers that "the people of the surrounding country are very much exasperated at this wanton violation of our territory, and earnestly besought Col. Many to dispatch troops immediately to that place." Colonel Many took the report seriously enough that the next day, November 30, he left the fort at the head of a column of troops including companies D, E, F and K of the Third Regiment, representing a large percentage of the garrison. The Texans had crossed into United States territory in pursuit of some Caddo who had allegedly crossed into Texas to steal livestock. After disarming the band and threating the U.S. government's Indian agent to the Caddo for providing them with arms and ammunition, Rusk reentered Texas territory instead of risking an armed conflict with U.S. troops. This was another case of the garrison of Fort Jesup coming to the aid of a minority group, as the expectation would have been for them to side with the Texans instead of protecting the Caddo. The troops returned to Fort Jesup on December 15.[104]

In the January 8, 1839 issue of the *Army and Navy Chronicle*, part of a letter describing the layout and buildings of Fort Jesup was published:

We are situated in the midst of a dense forest, on an eminence, which alone has been cleared of its timber. The loftiest, and most ornamental trees, (chiefly oak) having been left standing, scattered here and there, around the buildings, and about the parade ground. The houses of the post are arranged in a rectangle, almost a square. They are painted white, are ornamented with balconies, piazzas, and pillars, and all face inward towards the area, which constitutes a grand parade ground. The officers' quarters are on the sides nearest the road, while the side opposite, with its two adjacent angles, are made up of the quarters of the men and their families. In the rear of each company's quarters, is a large garden, to each of which a gardener is appropriated.

Fort Jesup is 25 miles from Natchitoches, La., on the stage road to San Augustin[e] Texas, about 50 miles from the latter. The former is a beautiful town of some 3 or 4000 inhabitants, French and Americans principally. It is pleasantly situated, on the southern band of the Red river, 100 miles above Alexandria, and 4 or 500 above New Orleans. The river is thickly and richly settled all the way down, chiefly by French planters, some of whom are immensely wealthy. In short, this is a delightful country, with the finest possible climate, and watered by streams, navigable by steamboats, some of them thousands of miles.

Fort Jesup is said to be one of the healthiest and most pleasant posts in the country. We have a large store, a post office, and on the opposite side of the road, a well ordered, quiet hotel. The officers seldom visit it, and the soldiers are not allowed to. Outside, and opposite the garrison, stands an elegant, and well appointed dwelling—the quarters of the commanding officer.

As to the facilities for reading, &c., we have a large reading-room, containing an extensive, well selected library, with newspapers from every part of the United States. The expense is defrayed from the post fund, and every one at the garrison has access to it. Over this hall, are four neat, well furnished rooms, with doors opening on galleries, both in front and rear, which are occupied by the four only bachelor saints, of whom your humble servant, unfortunately is one.

Several of the older officers have families, and have resided here for years. There is a school for the children, and by the late act of congress, we are provided with a chaplain. Most of the officers are temperance men to the hilt; saving a little wine occasionally, they drink nothing but cold water.[105]

Another article about Fort Jesup appeared in *Army and Navy Chronicle* on Thursday, September 12, 1839:

> *Fort Jesup—The Natchitoches Herald describes this military post as a very agreeable spot, and quite eligible as a summer retreat for those living in sickly sections of the state. On account of its location, equidistant from the Red river and the Sabine, on the ridge which divides those streams, with no low grounds for miles around, the healthiness of the place for many years past is not surpassed by any military post in the union. It has attractions, too, independent of the important one of health, which makes it a most delightful resort in summer, as indeed it is at all seasons of the year. Among them is noticed its cultivated and polished society, its beautiful groves and gardens, its fine band of music, fine water, fine hotel, fine landlord—its delicious breezes, that come sweeping over the pineclad hills. These are some of the fine and delightful things that are to be met with at Fort Jesup.*[106]

Unfortunately, the pleasant routine of life at Fort Jesup was about to be broken by events in the Florida War. For the first several years of the Seminole War, the strategy had been to use large groups of militia and volunteers supported by regular army units (mostly artillery units trained and armed as infantry), but as the war progressed, it became apparent that short-term volunteers were not suited for the hardships of the campaign. Even after Congress increased the size of the regular army, it was still difficult to field a large enough professional force, so the War Department began shifting more and more troops from the western frontier to Florida, as well as splitting regiments even further to try and maintain the posts along the frontier. At first, the reductions had only a small effect on Fort Jesup. From January 1839 to November 1839, the post's garrison grew from 200 soldiers to over 330. However, in December 1839, the garrison was reduced to 116 officers and men, as 217 soldiers from Companies I, F and K of the Third Infantry left Fort Jesup on December 13 for Fort Gibson to replace troops deployed from there. As more of the Third Infantry were sent to Florida, Company G, Fourth Infantry, was transferred to Fort Jesup. The fort remained the headquarters of the Third Infantry, and the garrison increased from 120 men in January to 200 by July 1840.

However, by 1840, military planners completely changed tactics in Florida. Attempts to draw the Seminoles into a major battle were abandoned. Instead, the territory was divided into zones with a supply base in the middle of each zone, and a series of roads was built, allowing the fast deployment of troops and supplies both within each zone and between zones. Discarding traditional methods, officers reshaped their commands into small, fast-moving units able to patrol assigned areas and push the Seminoles farther into the swamps. Another change in tactics was shifting to year-round campaigning. In the nineteenth century, most armies fought during the spring and summer, with some combat in early fall. However, due to the extreme heat, humidity and high rate of disease in the tropical Florida climate, the army stayed in camp most of the summer and fought in the winter. The Seminoles quickly learned this pattern and spent the summer planting crops and storing supplies. After 1840, the army would not give the Seminoles a chance to rest and resupply; instead, the army would hunt the Seminoles year-round. Very few volunteer units were used; instead, the burden of year-round warfare fell heaviest on the regular army. To meet the manpower needs for year-round warfare, the remaining troops on the frontier were rushed to Florida, leaving only small caretaking units at the frontier forts, so in 1840, it was decided to rotate the headquarters of the Third Infantry to Florida, beginning in October. By November 1840, the garrison of Fort Jesup was reduced to sixty-four men and placed under the command of Captain P. Morrison of Company G, Fourth Infantry.[107]

Fearing starvation even more than bullets, several of the holdout Seminole bands finally surrendered and agreed to be removed. A few bands refused to come out of hiding and would cause the Third Seminole War a decade later (1855–58). The Second Seminole War would claim the lives of over 1,500 soldiers and cost an estimated $15 million. Of the infantry units deployed to Florida that had been stationed at Fort Jesup, the Third Infantry lost 3 officers and 65 men, the Fourth lost 6 officers and 128 men, the Sixth lost 10 officers and 128 men and the Seventh lost 4 officers and 116 men.[108] When Dr. Jarvis, one of the doctors who served with the Sixth Infantry in 1836, returned to the site of Camp Sabine in 1844, he summed up the feelings of many military men in a letter to his brother when he wrote:

I spent an hour in melancholy reflections on the changes in the fate and fortune of the officers with whom I associated at this place in 1836.… Death has made sad havoc with them since that period and the solemn meaning of the wind thro' the tall pines that surrounded it seemed still more to sadden my feelings. Out of the 22 officers of the 6th Infy. stationed there at the time, nine are dead and the greater part of the remainder resigned. Nearly all the former were kill'd or died in Florida.

Poor fellows! They little dreamst [sic] *during the fun and frolic at that time that Death would in the course of one short year make such havoc in their ranks. The Seminole rifle and a Florida fever were alike certain of their victims, and regardless of rank.*[109]

After the war, the Western Department was reorganized, the Third Infantry was sent to Jefferson Barracks and the Second Dragoons would be sent to Fort Jesup. The end of the war, combined with an economic depression that started in 1837, also brought cuts to the military budget, a reduction in the number of soldiers and uncertainty over which units would be disbanded. The Second Dragoons were sent to Fort Jesup to "rest" after almost six years of combat duty, but their time there would not be as peaceful as hoped, and within three years, they were preparing for another war.

CHAPTER 7

THE SECOND DRAGOONS AT FORT JESUP

After the end of hostilities in the Florida War, the army was reorganized again. Units were reduced in size, regiments were reassigned and talk began of cutting several regiments, including all the mounted forces. Most of the companies of the Second Dragoons, which had served in Florida since its creation in 1836, were sent to Fort Jesup. The first five companies arrived at the post on January 14, 1842, and the post again became a regimental headquarters. Although the Second Dragoons had an uncertain future, it had a proud past and a well-deserved reputation as a hard-fighting unit, a reputation that would be honed on the parade ground at Fort Jesup.

The perceived cost of mounted units (feeding, caring for and housing both the horse and the soldier) made them an easy target for nineteenth-century politicians wanting to balance the federal budget on the backs of the military and led to the long and, at times, confusing road to the creation of the Second Dragoons. As was typical of American military policy, after the War of 1812 was won, the size of the army was cut, and one of the casualties was all the mounted units of the cavalry. It would be seventeen years before the United States again fielded anything close to a mounted regiment. In 1832, attempting to meet the need for mounted troops while limiting military spending, Congress created the Regiment of Mounted Rangers, a volunteer force recruited for one-year terms of service, and required the rangers to provide their own horses, rifles, clothing and equipment. Unfortunately, their clothing and appearance, while well suited for the rigors of frontier service, could not awe anyone, and the Indians often mistook them for traders or common militia. They were disbanded after one year. Congress authorized the creation of the Regiment of Dragoons on March 2, 1833, and after being trained and outfitted, the regiment was spread out between Fort Gibson and Leavenworth and, later, Fort Scott, but it was obvious that a single regiment could not cover the massive expansions of the West. With a full-scale Indian war breaking out in Florida, and the possibility of conflict in both Texas and the Indian territory, Congress voted to expand the army by creating an additional infantry regiment and the Second Regiment of Dragoons on May 23, 1836. However, instead of being deployed to the Great Plains, the dragoons were sent to the swamps of Florida, and the troopers would spend the next seven years wading through the swamps, fighting an elusive enemy.[110]

Near the end of the conflict in Florida, the dragoons received word that most of the regiment had been ordered to Fort Jesup. Five companies would be departing immediately; the other companies would leave later. The first five companies left Florida on horseback and rode to Baton Rouge, where, on January 2, 1842, the dragoons boarded a steamer to travel up the Mississippi River to the Red River and disembarked at Grand Ecore. On January 14, the Second Dragoons paraded through the streets of Natchitoches, then turned and marched down the old El Camino Real toward their new post and home. But for two of the officers of the regiment, this march would bring back memories of the march of the Seventh Infantry twenty years earlier. The commander of the regiment, fifty-two-year-old Colonel David E. Twiggs, had been a company commander on the first march to Fort Jesup in 1822, and regimental adjutant Lieutenant Henry Hopkins Sibley had been a young boy watching Taylor's troops march through the town. Sibley grew up in Natchitoches and was the brother-in-law to Francis Lee, who was post quartermaster at various times in the 1820s and 1830s. He often visited the home of the Lee family at Fort Jesup and even moved in with them around Christmas 1832, before he left for West Point. After graduation, Sibley was assigned as regimental adjutant while the regiment was still in Florida.[111]

David E. Twiggs was a veteran officer who had served at Fort Jesup as a company commander when the post was established. George Ballentine, who served under General Twiggs during the Mexican-American War, described him as:

In height the general is about 5 feet, 10 inches, very broad shouldered and bull necked, and is altogether a very stout and robust looking man, though verging on 60 years of age. His face is large and red, with blue eyes, and rather coarse and heavy looking features; an exuberant mass of tow white hair, with long beard, and whiskers of the same color, giving him a gruff appearance, quite in keeping with his character, in which the disagreeable and unprepossessing are the preponderating qualities. But he was a great favorite among the men, who admired him principally, I believe, for his brusquerie [sic] and coarseness of manner, and a singular habit he had of swearing most vehemently, and flying into a passion on the most trifling occasions. But though General Twiggs had the most republican contempt for etiquette, and even the common courtesies of civilized life, in his intercourse with others, he was furious if a soldier happened to omit paying him the customary military salute in passing[112]

When the troopers arrived at Fort Jesup, Twiggs was not pleased with the condition in which he found his new command. He reported to Jesup that "the Officers' Quarters at this post are nearly falling down, in fact not a single building except the four company quarters and the kitchens to those quarters and one house built" were in good repair. Fort Jesup, like most of the army, had fallen on hard times because of the cost of the Second Seminole War and the Panic of 1837. Many of the repairs and expansions that had been planned had been put on hold by Congress. Even if money had been available, there was simply too much repair work for the small caretaker garrison to keep up with. Many of the buildings had not been occupied for a year or more after the Third Infantry left for Florida. Twiggs was horrified at the condition of the post but understood the difficulties the caretaker garrison had, writing that "I have never seen such a dilapidated post since I have been in the army and from no neglect of the Commg [sic] Officer but it appears the work of time."[113]

Converting Fort Jesup from an infantry station to a cavalry station presented many problems, including the need for new storehouses to hold supplies for both the soldiers and their horses, as well as the problem of hauling supplies (especially hay for the horses). The forage and property storehouses (built around 1834 or 1835), including the granary, hay house, stables, wagon house and other buildings, were found to be "totally inadequate to the protection of their contents from the effects of the weather." The buildings were also too small for the needs of the new garrison, having been built for the needs of the handful of animals used by the quartermaster's department, and had to be rebuilt. As far as stables for the roughly two hundred dragoon horses, there were none. Colonel Twiggs ordered temporary stables be set up under the soldiers' barracks until suitable stables could be constructed.[114]

After seven years of active campaigning in the swamps and tropical climate of Florida, the men of the Second Dragoons were in almost as bad shape as the buildings at Fort Jesup. Dr. Jarvis wrote, "My hospital is constantly fill'd with sick and those broken down in Florida service." Three dragoons died at the post between their arrival and March 31, 1842; two died from disease, and one took his own life by shooting himself in the head with his carbine. Ordnance Sergeant Detmore also passed away on March 31, 1842, after being sick for several days.[115]

David Twiggs. *Library of Congress.*

After the regiment had settled into its new home, Colonel Twiggs began an extensive training program, largely overseen by William J. Hardee, who had spent time in Europe studying the latest developments in cavalry tactics. Hardee personally trained the officers in the use of sabers and ensured that the officers trained their troopers to the highest standards. Two squadrons were trained as lancers, and not only would they have created an impressive scene with their tall spears, created at the post, but they were also the only lancers in the entire United States regular army. As one early historian and former member of the Second recalled: "If the 'Second' acquired a reputation for courage and endurance in Florida, its early proficiency in drill and its proverbially good discipline were gained at 'Jesup,' in the seventh year of its existence as an organization."[116]

As early as January 1839, Colonel Many requested that a sawmill be purchased for the fort, to no avail. When the Second Dragoons arrived at Fort Jesup, Twiggs continued to request a sawmill be purchased. Twiggs felt that "logs either hewed or round are the very worst houses for the South, they decay in twelve or eighteen months and cannot be otherwise than very unhealthy and the labour [*sic*] of erecting them is more than twice that of frame." He reported that there were four new company quarters and that if the sawmill was supplied, the rest of the buildings could be built for $10,000, considerably cheaper than building them out of hewn logs. In July 1842, Thomas Jesup ordered Captain Cross to purchase a steam-powered sawmill from New Orleans for Fort Jesup. The sawmill arrived around July 9, 1842, and Twiggs quickly put it to work. Unfortunately, and to Twiggs's anger and frustration, "the mechanic employed did not understand his business and failed in his part of the machinery." Even as late as November, the mill was still not sawing at full speed, but Twiggs held out hope that with a few repairs, the mill could saw over one thousand feet of lumber a day. He also requested permission to begin constructing new buildings at the post, because "the buildings are almost tumbling down." Orders approving the construction and repair projects were received on November 26, 1842, and work continued through the spring and summer. By February, the issues with the sawmill had been solved, and it was able to cut one hundred feet an hour.[117]

With the construction of new officers' quarters came the problem of whom they would be assigned to. The military assigned quarters to officers based on their seniority and not on the size of their families, and anytime a new officer of a higher rank arrived on a post or new quarters were built, a higher-ranking officer could claim the quarters of a lower-ranking officer and force him to move, even if he had been in the quarters for years. This started a chain reaction of lower-ranking officers having to claim new quarters and forcing other lower-ranking officers to move. Sometimes, the officers of the post agreed to let an officer with a larger family have bigger quarters, but there was no policy officially allowing this, and any senior officer could nullify the agreement and claim the larger quarters. The one thing an officer could not do was claim more rooms then allowed by regulation. Apparently, in February 1843, there was a dispute over how many rooms an officer could claim. Captain Graham moved into one of the new officers' quarters buildings, which contained ten rooms, including the two kitchens and the upper rooms which were heated by a stove, adding to the livable space. Graham claimed the entire building due to his higher rank, and in the process, Brevet Captain R.A. Arnold and his family were evicted. Adding insult to injury was the fact that while Graham was single, Arnold had the second-largest family on post. In February 1844, Arnold, through Post Quartermaster Dix, requested a ruling on the matter from General Jesup. Dix reported the building was designed to house two captains or four lieutenants, stating that the building had "2 kitchens and 2 servants' rooms, as well as 2 parlor rooms 20 feet square, with two attic rooms…of the same dimensions as the parlors" and two small rooms (12 by 15 feet) adjoining the parlors, which made the building larger than a captain's allowance. Jesup ruled that an officer could not claim more than his allowance for quarters, the building had to be shared and any excess rooms should be distributed so "as to offer the greatest degree of comfort to all."[118]

Rumors were spreading in the summer of 1842 that the Dragoons were to be disbanded as Congress attempted to reduce military spending at the end of the Second Seminole War. If the Dragoons were disbanded, Twiggs swore "to leave everything in as good order as possible and shall up to the moment of my leaving secure every department here." When the additional three companies sent from Florida through Baton Rouge arrived, he set them to work building stables for their horses, which were finished before August 30. He also asked that if the regiment were disbanded, the men be sent to a station north of Charleston to be discharged, due to the "feeble health, many of them from long service in Florida" and the cost of transportation, which would be less expensive from a northern post, about thirty dollars per man, compared to eighty dollars per man. He suggested that the horses could be sold in New Orleans for a better price, the average price per horse being about twenty dollars if they were sold from the fort. As to the officers, Twiggs reported that "I have nothing to complain of. We all knew our commissions were held at the pleasure of Congress."[119]

Instead of disbanding the regiment, Congress voted in the spring of 1843 to dismount the Second Dragoons and convert them to a rifle regiment. On March 13, 1843, General Order 22 was issued, outlining that the Second was to send what horses were in a healthy condition to the First Dragoons and that those not fit for service should be turned over to the quartermaster's department to be sold. Carbines and sabers would be replaced by rifles, and until a new uniform was designed, the regiment was to keep its current uniforms. The unit was to be redesignated as the United States Rifle Regiment.[120]

Twiggs reported that on March 24, 1843, the dragoon's horses were turned over to the quartermaster's department to be sold. Two hundred horses were sold at the auction that took place on May 1, which "attracted a great number of person here from a distance and the prices at which they sold were high (averaging $42 a piece) considering the scarcity of money and the age of the horses, most of them having been purchased in 1836 when the regt. [sic] was first mounted and had served thro all the campaigns in Fa." Officers who had accompanied the dragoons from Florida to the western frontier were allowed to keep some of the horses at the rate of three for field officers and two for company officers. This applied only to the dragoons' horses, not to other public horses on the fort, such as the quartermaster's department's horses. With their horses sold, the Rifle Regiment began the process of learning how to march and fight on foot. While officers and enlisted men maintained a sense of professionalism, their morale was noticeably lower, and they dreamed of the day when they would be remounted.[121]

One would think that with as many armed soldiers as Fort Jesup had, money would be safe there; however, on March 28, 1843, Private Charles Lovenshold of H Company, U.S. Riflemen, broke into the quarters of Lieutenant Torry, post commissary, and stole $2,300.65. Lovenshold was the commissary clerk, and during the day of March 27, while helping Torry count the money, he stole the extra key to the safe, which Torry normally kept locked in the safe. Lovenshold then broke into Torry's sleeping quarters, where the safe was kept, opened it with his key and made off with the money. Lovenshold was quickly captured and turned over to the civilian courts for trial. He pled guilty to the crime and was sentenced to two years' hard labor in the state penitentiary by the civilian court. A board of inquiry was convened at Fort Jesup by Twiggs, consisting of Major Fauntleroy, Dr. Jarvis and one other captain, on April 21, 1843, at three o'clock, to determine the responsibility of Torry in the matter. The board found that "Lt. Torry is a person of business habits and particularly careful of public property entrusted to his charge. Also, that the Iron Safe in which his public funds are deposited is placed in his sleeping apartment." The board also reported that he "was in the constant habit of carrying the key of the Iron Safe about his person." The board was of the "opinion that no blame can be attached to Lieut Torry for said robbery."[122]

Dr. Jarvis wrote in a letter that

> *some time last month a soldier performing the duties of Commissary Clerk became infected with the spirt of the times and the example of greater men swartwonted* [sic] *or absquatulated* [sic] *or carried off $2000 public monies in gold and silver belonging to the Commissary which he abstracted from the iron chest, having obtained a duplicate key to the same. He immediately took the Sabine chute or in other words eloped for Texas, but it was a week before his course was discovered, the impression being at first that he had gone to* [New Orleans] *whither the commissary went in pursuit of him, of course without success. As soon as it was discovered he had gone to Texas, an officer with two men went in pursuit & fortunately apprehended him in Houston and brot* [sic] *him back, but unfortunately found no money. He stated that 3 men stopped him on the road & robbed him shortly after he got in Texas. In that rascally country there is not even honor among thieves, as you see they rob each other. The absquatulating clerk was carried to Natchitoches jail & handed over to the civil authorities for punishment.*[123]

Although the Second Dragoons were sent to Fort Jesup in part to rest and recover from their service in the Second Seminole War, they spent a great deal of their time during the first two years repairing and rebuilding the post. Despite the poor condition of the post when the dragoons arrived, they soon restored it to a position of health and comfort. Before long, the post could boast of "substantial quarters for officers and men, spacious parade and drill ground, and every convenience for comfort and amusement possible to procure on the frontier. There was a theatre and a gymnasium ably supported by the men, under the patronage of the officers, a school, a chapel, and…a sutler's store, filled with most attractive wares."[124] In the vicinity of the post were "billiard tables, ninepin alleys, ball alleys, a theatre, and shops kept by citizens [in] which liquors are sold to all who call for them, be they soldiers or citizens."[125]

Unlike previous post commanders, Twiggs allowed his men to visit the local establishments and purchase alcohol as a reward for good service. Inspector general George Croghan wrote in his May 14, 1844 inspection report that: "I have never before seen so fine a command, and I question whether a better in every respect is to be found anywhere. Discipline the most perfect prevails throughout, and that too, as some will have it, under every discouragement, as all around are lures to draw a soldier away from his duty." Croghan thought that it was because Twiggs treated the soldiers "as men in whom confidence may be placed, and they take pride in proving to their officers that they have not overestimated their worth." Twiggs felt that if he went back to a system of trying to stop all of his soldiers from drinking, he would have one-third "drunk in a week," but by using the freedom to purchase alcohol as a motivation, he was able to help prevent drunkenness. Not everyone praised Twiggs's ideas as highly as Croghan. Dr. Jarvis, a member of the temperance movement, felt that "the way they drink whiskey would astound a member of the temperance society. Col. Twiggs gives them permission to drink as much as they please and to ev'ryone that asks it, establish groggeries when and where they please. He goes in direct opposition to all the notions of discipline, police and military duty entertained and practiced by all commanding officers of the present day or at any previous period, and contrary to the experience of all."[126]

As the number of soldiers at the post grew, so did the number of civilians in the area trying to provide places for the soldiers to spend their pay. Jarvis wrote in May 1843 that

> *Fort Jesup bears resemblance already to a city, if not in the size at least in the nature & character of its amusements and the variety of the genus homo. We have performances in the theater 3 times a week which generally*

has an audience of 200 persons and in addition to this, last week we had the performance of a circus belonging to Welsh and Co. of N.Y. They had just arrived from Mexico and Texas and in addition to the amusements of the ring in which there was some excellent riding, were the performances of the India rubber man as he is call'd who apparently has no bones in his body and can perform as many contortions with his limbs as an eel and walking with as much apparent ease with his legs crossed behind his neck, his head downwards, as one can in an upright position, and very much resembling a species of crab call'd fiddlers which you have doubtless seen on the shores of Tampa Bay. The wonder and surprise seemed to be equally divided between his feats and those of a monstrous baboon, one of the most horrible animals I ever beheld. The latter rode a beautiful Shetland pony about 26 inches in height. A juggler arrived about the same time and opened his performance which of course were varied and extremely well done, nearly equal to Signior Blits or Adrien, or Mr. Winchall. The other places of resort & amusement are 2 billiard rooms, 2 ten pin alleys, 3 taverns and grogeries [sic] innumerable. To support them we have all description of characters including horse jockeys, blacklags, loafers, etc. All these places have been erected & these characters suffered to remain by permission of Col. Twiggs who seems to have the ambition of founding a second Rome from the vilest materials.[127]

National events would again end the peacefulness of Fort Jesup, as affairs in Texas would soon put the post back in the national spotlight. The quiet routines of a frontier fort were replaced with preparations for the impending Mexican-American War. The dragoons, who were sent to Fort Jesup to recover from the last war, would soon find themselves preparing for another, as the garrison was augmented by the Third Infantry and Fourth Infantry and the arrival of the new theater commander, Zachary Taylor.

CHAPTER 8

THE EVE OF WAR

Although it had taken about twenty years, the purpose for Fort Jesup that General Gaines had foreseen had come to pass. The fort was in the national spotlight again, and it was about to begin its most important role. It would become, once again, the headquarters of a military district, as well as headquarters of the Army of Observation (about one-quarter of the active U.S. Army). General Gaines had predicted in 1822 that at some point, the U.S. Army would march into Texas and that Fort Jesup would serve as a major staging and training ground, and he was proven correct. The army that left Fort Jesup was one of the most well-trained, well-disciplined and professional fighting forces in American history, and for the first time in American history, the U.S. Army was prepared to fight and win a war before it began.

Even before Texas won its independence, there were elements in the United States that wanted to make Texas a state. After the Texas victory in 1836, negotiations began to bring the new republic into the Union, but two issues would haunt the negotiations for almost a decade. The first was the fact that Mexico never recognized the independence of Texas and on multiple occasions threatened to declare war on the United States if they tried to annex the wayward province. The second was the growing controversy over slavery, and the issue quickly became involved in the politics of annexation. Northern politicians feared that Texas would be admitted as a proslavery state, changing the balance of votes in the House of Representatives and the Senate. There was also no guarantee that Texas would choose to join the United States, as both England and France were actively courting the new country, offering protection from both Mexico and Native Americans in exchange for cotton and other economic incentives.

By the fall of 1843, Secretary of State Abel P. Upshur opened a new series of negotiations with Texas, and by mid-February 1844, the talks had moved close enough to an agreement that Texas requested a naval force be stationed in the Gulf and a large military force be stationed close enough to Texas that if Mexico invaded Texas to prevent annexation, the United States would be ready to intervene. The War Department issued orders to transfer units to Louisiana and, on April 23, directed Zachary Taylor to assume command of the First Military District and move the headquarters of the district from Baton Rouge to Fort Jesup. While there were higher-ranking officers available, Winfield Scott (who never publicly explained his reasons) probably felt that Taylor was the most senior officer physically capable of commanding the troops in the field. Taylor was also familiar with the area, having spent time commanding various posts in Louisiana, including Baton Rouge and Fort Jesup. Taylor's command was first referred to as the Corps of Observation and was not considered to be under General Gaines, who commanded the Western Department of the army. In fact, Taylor was ordered to open confidential correspondence with Texas president Sam Houston but was under orders not to share the details of the correspondence with Gaines. In the event of a Mexican invasion before the treaty was ratified, Taylor was to inform the Mexican commander that any incursion could be seen as an act of war against the United States once the treaty went into effect.[128]

One advantage of the possibility of conflict with Mexico was the remounting of the Second Dragoons in the spring of 1844. Lobbying to remount the regiment by both the War Department and the Louisiana and Missouri delegations to Congress had started almost immediately after the order came to dismount the troops. On March 4, 1844, a bill was passed in the House to remount the regiment, and when a similar bill passed the Senate, the regiment was authorized to again become mounted soldiers. When word reached the garrison of their return to horse soldier status, an impromptu celebration broke out. All duties except for guard duty were canceled, and each enlisted man was given an extra gill of whiskey. Officers, too, had a celebration, and soon it was decided that a "mounted" salute would be fired. Two officers (referred to in the earliest regimental history, *From Everglade to Canyon*, as Captains M— and G— but most likely Captains Graham and May) were selected to mount the cannon that had already been loaded for the evening salute. The other officers around the cannon started jockeying for the honor to pull the lanyard. Soon, the horseplay caused Captain G— to shift too far back, and he wound up over the venthole. Each dragoon officer and enlisted man had an addition to their uniforms that infantry did not need, the "reinforce": a diamond-shaped piece of material that was sewn onto the seat of the breeches between the legs of the mounted soldier so that, as he rode a horse all day, his pants would not wear out as fast. When the lanyard was pulled, a column of hot gases and flame shot up from the venthole and the men heard "a slight swear, almost drowned in the shrieks of laughter, which greeted poor G— as he emerged from the ordeal of saltpeter, with his best stable-jacket in flames and the 'reinforce' of his light-blue breeches not so apparent as it had been. With no gentle hand he was rolled over and over in the grass until, no longer a dashing cavalier, but a melancholy and smoldering ruin."[129]

Orders quickly went out to frontier posts informing them of which units would be sent to Fort Jesup. Making provisions for the increases in the size of the garrison, Twiggs ordered that the sawmill be kept working cutting planks, which could be used by the soldiers to make floors for their tents, providing some level of comfort. On April 20, 1844, Major Hitchcock of the Third Infantry received word that he and his regiment were being sent from Jefferson Barracks to Fort Jesup and recorded in his diary:

> Great excitement today. As I returned to garrison after retreat, I was met by Captain Larnard and saluted with the news that my regiment is ordered to Fort Jesup, Louisiana. Quite unexpected. Rumors are rife of the annexation of Texas, and this may be movement towards making a military occupancy of the country beyond the Sabine. I may make the first move into Texas with the colors of the United States, but I am convinced I shall not make the last.
>
> Hasty measures of preparation were taken; books were stored; property not needed was hurriedly sold; farewell dinners were given and calls of courtesy were made; an impromptu dance was had; some tears were shed by sweethearts and acquaintances....
>
> Sunday, 28th April. Farewell books—study—etc. Goodbye Plato, and all the rest! We are on board the 1400-ton steamboat Maria, and leaving behind us the lowering clouds of yesterday.[130]

The regiment arrived at the mouth of the Red River on May 3 and the next day was transferred to the steamer *Beeswing* and proceeded up the river to Natchitoches. Two days later, the men arrived at the small port town of

Left: Ethan Allen Hitchcock. *Library of Congress.*

Below: Park volunteers portraying a scene at a typical army camp in 1845. *Photo by author.*

Grand Ecore (the main port for the city of Natchitoches after the Red River changed its course).[131]

A few days after the Third left Jefferson Barracks, the Fourth Infantry also received orders to proceed to Louisiana. One of the members of the regiment was a young, lovestruck lieutenant, Ulysses Grant. Grant had been stationed at Jefferson Barracks since his graduation from West Point and, during that time, had fallen in love with the sister of one of his military academy classmates, Julia Dent. Before the regiment was sent to the frontier, the two young people enjoyed each other's company, but it was not until their separation that the two realized they were in love. Grant was on leave when his regiment was sent to Louisiana (visiting his parents in Ohio), so after he reported back at the end of his leave, he mounted a horse and rode to join his regiment.[132]

While the Third set up camp near Fort Jesup, the Fourth "selected a place in the pine woods, between the old town of Natchitoches and Grand Ecore, about three miles from each and on high ground back from the river." The place was given the name Camp Salubrity and proved entitled to it. The camp was on "a high, sandy pine ridge, which caught the breezes off the river, and with spring branches in the valley, in the front and rear of the camp. The springs furnished an abundance of cool, pure water, and the ridge was above the flight of mosquitoes, which abound in that region in great multitudes. In the valley they swarmed in myriads, but never came to the summit of the ridge. The regiment occupied this camp six months before the first death occurred, and that was caused by an accident." When Grant arrived at Natchitoches, he chose to make the three-mile uphill hike to the encampment rather than use one of the local wagon drivers who had set up taxi services at an exorbitant rate.[133]

The officers and men of the Fourth were housed in tents, and as the summer heat increased, sheds were built over the tents to provide shade. Grant recalled that "the summer was whiled away in social enjoyments among the officers, in visiting those stationed at, and near, Fort Jesup, twenty-five miles away, visiting the planters on the Red River and the citizens of Natchitoches and Grand Encore [sic]." Cards and gambling were a major pastime for the officers and soldiers while they were waiting for word on the treaty negotiations, although young Grant apparently had no talent for cards and lost money every time he sat down at a game. His lack of card skills was more than made up for by his skill at horse riding. He bought a fine thoroughbred and rode it in local races. Grant was often invited into plantation homes to talk horses and tour stables.[134]

One of the new arrivals to Fort Jesup was Private Upton of the Third Infantry, who described his voyage from a training center to the fort in a letter to his father:

> *We had a long, though on the whole quite a pleasant passage to New Orleans. We were twenty days on the ship. We stopped at New Orleans Barracks three or four days, then took a steamboat for Natchitoches which took about three and a half days. A march of four miles brought us to Fort Salubrious [sic] (Camp Suliberty) where the Forth Regiment lays. We rested a day or two, then marched twenty five miles which brought us to our journeys end, viz, Fort Jesup.*
>
> *We were marched, 190 in number, on the morning of the third of March to the wharf and got on board a little schooner which took us to the ship one mile to North East, from which quarter a smart breeze was blowing. After beating about an hour and a half we reached the ship. She was a large new cream colored packet ship, the nicest I had ever seen. After selecting a berth and putting my knapsack in it, I went above to make an observation of matters and things in general. The Captain was heard giving curious, and of course to me perfectly incomprehensible, orders to the sailors, but I could see the effects of them, for while some were hauling down the sail others were drawing up the anchors with a machine that works like a fire engine. Soon the sails filled, the anchors hoisted to their places, and the gallant ship was moving through the waters like a thing of life.*[135]

General Taylor arrived at Fort Jesup on June 18, 1844, and assumed command of the military department. Under Taylor's command would be eight companies of the Third and eight companies of the Fourth Regiments of Infantry and the Second Dragoons. In total, Taylor had roughly 1,090 soldiers under his direct command, a large number considering that the entire U.S. Army only had an authorized strength of 8,619 officers and men and, of that number, only about 6,562 men of all ranks were present for duty. Named the Army of Observation, Taylor's force represented the largest gathering of regular troops in over twenty years.[136]

However, even before Taylor arrived at Fort Jesup, the treaty to annex Texas was defeated in the Senate. The War Department, not sure how to proceed, decided on a "wait and see" approach, leaving the troops on the border, with no instructions or clear plan, to wait for the pro-annexation movement to make its next move. Taylor was ordered to remain at Fort Jesup but cease all correspondence with the Texas government.[137]

The failure to ratify the treaty did not calm things down on the frontier; in fact, they became more heated. On June 19, Mexican general Adrian Woll, who commanded the Mexican Army along the Rio Grande, informed Texas president Sam Houston that his government no longer intended to honor the armistice between the two counties. Reports spread throughout Texas and the United States that Mexico was assembling a force of over six hundred soldiers on the Rio Grande to attack San Antonio, and there were reports of Mexican agents encouraging Native tribes to attack Texas settlements.[138]

Taylor and his regimental commanders soon found themselves in the difficult position of maintaining a readiness to move at a moment's notice, while having to prepare for the possibility of remaining along the border for an extended period. It was necessary to continue to make repairs to the buildings and, in some cases, build new ones. Between April 30 and October 7, 1844, two new buildings were built at the fort. The first was a new adjutant's office that was "[frame] and weather boarded with 3 brick chimnies [sic], with 2 rooms that were 20 feet square and 2 rooms that were 12 by 15 feet with a twelve foot wide piazza in front. The second was a frame building for the use of the band. It was 20 feet by 16 feet with a 9 foot wide piazza in front and one brick chimney."[139]

Park volunteers demonstrating how soldiers would have made shingles for their buildings. *Photo by author.*

With the remounting of the Second Dragoons, new stables had to be built to house the horses, since the stables built in 1842 had been torn down and the materials used for other repairs when the horses were sold in 1843, even though no one knew how long the troops would be staying at the fort. On March 27, 1845, Twiggs ordered Captain Dix to begin gathering the tools and supplies necessary to build new stables for the seven companies of dragoons at the post. Twiggs reported on April 10 that "in five or six days we shall have completed stables for seven companies. They are not so fine as other corps have but they have one recommendation. They were built without expense to the United States except a few nails." Twiggs wrote on April 14 that "on Saturday next the 19th we shall have complete for each Dragoon company at this post, stables, and forage houses.…The stables are as good as I ever want on this frontier." The stables were finished just in time, because on April 19, the first 150 horses needed to remount the regiment arrived. As Twiggs reported, "We were taken by surprise. Only having about three hours' notice that they were on the way." This raised all kinds of issues because there was "no horse equipment at the post and not a curry comb or brush." There was also no forage for the horses at the fort, and no local source could provide enough, so food had to be purchased along the western frontier and sent to Grand Ecore, which was cheaper than buying it through New Orleans and paying the cost of shipping from the East Coast. The officers were given first choice of the horses and paid the contractor directly; the remaining 143 horses were paid for by the government for the soldiers. All were described as "of a very good quality."[140]

While negotiations remained stalled in the Senate, Taylor received instructions from the adjutant general like those given to General Gaines during the 1836 border crisis, including orders to be prepared to move in case the "Indians" or some other threat to the safety of the frontier should arise. Both Taylor and Hitchcock believed that the threat of an Indian war might be used as an excuse to move the army into Texas before the treaty was ratified, and they were outraged. It was one thing to cross into Texas if the elected officials of both countries voted to approve it, but the idea that the army would be used for some type of a backdoor political move pushed by a few members of the administration enraged the two officers. While they continued to make preparations for war, there were no plans to advance the army without orders or a confirmed tribal uprising.[141]

As summer turned into fall, preparations for war continued, but there was little communication between the War Department and the Army of Observation. Before winter weather hit, commanders of both the Third and Fourth Infantries prepared their troops for winter quarters. Hitchcock recorded in his journal: "15ᵗʰ October. Preparations going on for the march. But I am hutting the regiment for cold weather, notwithstanding, for we may possibly remain here all winter."[142] Adding to the comfort of the camp for the officers of the Fourth Infantry was the hiring of a local woman to handle the cooking. Grant and a fellow officer also hired a free person of color named Valere, who spoke English, French and Spanish, as a servant.[143] Grant recalled in his *Memoirs* that

> *as summer wore away, and colder nights came upon us, the tents we were occupying ceased to afford comfortable quarters; and "further orders" not reaching us, we began to look about to remedy the hardship. Men were put to work getting out timber to build huts, and in a very short time all were comfortably housed—privates as well as officers. The outlay by the government in accomplishing this was nothing, or nearly nothing. The winter was spent more agreeably than the summer had been. There were occasional parties given by the planters along the "coast"—as the bottom lands on the Red River were called. The climate was delightful.*[144]

In a December 1, 1844 letter, Grant wrote to his friend Lieutenant Hazlett about the "state of excitement under which the men were laboring, for they expected daily to be hurried off to the Texas Frontier," describing how all supplies not absolutely necessary were packed and stored at Grand Ecore, ready for transport on short notice. Grant also recalled the "muttered curses heaped upon the heads of the regimental officers who put the men at work building two long lines of blockhouses as winter quarters more comfortable than tents, when the men believed such labor unnecessary, in view of the expected early departure." Grant also recalled,

> *There were five days of races at Natchitoches. I was there every day and bet low, generally lost. Jarvis and a number from Jesup were there. Jarvis was pretty high and tried to be smart most of the time. He fell over the back of a bench at the race course and tumbled over backward in his chair in front of Thompson's Hotel during his most brilliant day. He undertook to play brag at our camp and soon succeeded in ridding himself of twenty dollars, all in quarters. The game of brag is kept up as lively as ever, I continued to play some after you left and won considerable, but for some time back I have not played and probably will never play again—no resolution though!*[145]

Both Christmas and New Year's came and went with no word on when or if the troops would be deployed. Hitchcock wrote:

> *January 1st 1845. New Year's Day. Still at Camp Wilkins, the name I gave to the camp of the 3rd Regiment of Infantry, adjacent to Fort Jesup. Colonel Twigg's and Regiment of Dragoons is in the barracks at the so-called Fort—there is nothing like a fort here….Some of our officers have been to a horse-race—others have witnessed that barbarous amusement, a dander-pulling. The ladies of camp have received calls. After mess I had a short ride on my bay Jim, and then took up the Meditations of Marcus Aurelius Antoninus, that heathen Spinoza.*
>
> *Evening. I came home and amused myself with the flute, playing the opera of Oberon and one or two others. Then I took a fancy to count my books and found 761, besides numerous pamphlets, magazines, and tracts, and also not including my music, of which I have over 60 volumes bound and enough music in sheets for 20 volumes more.*[146]

As winter turned to spring, Taylor was still in the dark over most of the political maneuvering related to the Texas issue. In fact, most of what Taylor knew of the situation came not from the War Department but from newspapers and travelers' reports, even though accurate information was vital to his ability as a theater commander to make plans for his troops. The overwhelming election of James K. Polk in 1844, who ran on a platform of expansion, reaffirmed the popularity of the annexation of Texas with the American people. When Congress met in December 1844, a joint resolution offering annexation to Texas was introduced. After months of debate, it passed both houses on March 1, 1845. Now the ball was in Texas's court, but annexation was not unanimously desired in Texas. In fact, Texas president Anson Jones favored continued independence and was working with Great Britain to negotiate a peace treaty between Mexico and Texas. However, Mexico continued to refuse to accept that Texas was no longer part of Mexico, and as these negotiations failed, more Texans began looking to foreign powers for protection—and not just the United States, but England and France as well, further complicating annexation. As the vote in Texas over annexation loomed closer and it began to look like annexation would be accepted, the Texas government asked for protection from U.S. troops against possible Mexican reprisals. With the arrival of the last two companies of the Third Infantry from Fort Leavenworth on April 23, Taylor's command included all ten companies of the Third

Infantry Regiment and seven companies of the Second Dragoons, plus eight companies of the Fourth Infantry at Camp Salubrity. On May 28, Secretary of War William L. Marcy issued a warning to Taylor to expect orders to move his troops into Texas very soon. On June 26, the Texas government formally asked for protection, and Taylor received orders on June 30, 1845, to move his force and advance into Texas. The Fourth was the first unit to advance, leaving camp on July 2 and arriving at Jackson Barracks in New Orleans two days later. The Third left on July 7 for New Orleans to travel to Corpus Christi, Texas, by steamer, and the Second Dragoons left on July 25 to march overland through Texas. Lieutenant Inge, acting assistant quartermaster, assumed command of the post on July 25 with a garrison of seventy-one men. Early Fort Jesup historian J. Fair Hardin may have painted the best mental image of the soldiers' departure when he wrote in the 1920s: "Thus the Army of Observation marched away to war from Fort Jesup and from Camp Salubrity, with bands playing, color flying, teamsters' oaths ringing, mule-skinners' long-whips cracking and clouds of dust rising from the long string of escort wagons along the old San Antonio Trace."[147]

The day the order to move was received, Hitchcock could barely contain his excitement and wrote in his journal:

> *Orders came last evening by express from Washington City directing General Taylor to move without any delay to some point on the coast near the Sabine or elsewhere, and as soon as he shall hear of the acceptance by Texas convention of the annexation resolutions of our Congress he is immediately to proceed with his whole command to the extreme western border of Texas and take up a position on the banks of or near the Rio Grande, and he is to expel an armed force of Mexicans who may cross that river. Bliss read the orders to me last evening hastily at tattoo. I have scarcely slept a wink, thinking of the needful preparations. I am now noting at reveille by candle-light and waiting the signal for muster....*
>
> *New Orleans, July 16, 1845. The 3rd Infantry under my command left Fort Jesup on Monday, the 7th at reveille, and marched that day sixteen miles towards Natchitoches. The next day marched to the river and embarked in two steamboats and arrived here without detention on the 10th.*[148]

Many of the soldiers in the army were excited about the upcoming war. For some, it was the sense of adventure; for others, it was a feeling of patriotism and helping America live up to its destiny; many were just happy to not have the mindless routines of garrison and fatigue duties. One of the soldiers under Hitchcock's command, Private Upton, recorded his departure in a letter to his friends on July 3:

> *I write a short letter today to inform you that I am well and that ere this reaches you, I shall be in Texas near the line of Mexico, where our regiment is ordered. The Third, Forth, and Sixth infantry are all ordered there, also the Second Dragoons. Everything is bustling, packing, and preparing for the march. All are eager to start, animation and enthusiasm is the order of the day.*
>
> *Our baggage is being sent to the steamboat landing at Natchitoches as fast as possible. We are to stop at the New Orleans Barracks to be joined by the Sixth Infantry and vessels are waiting at the mouth of the Mississippi to carry us where we are going. Where this place is I do not exactly know myself. We shall start from the post next Monday. There may be a chance of our having to burn a little powder in the face of the Mexicans yet. They appear to be determined to have a fuss.*[149]

As the infantry was preparing to enter Texas by sea, the dragoons began their preparations for an overland expedition through the newest state in the Union. The command that was readying to march included the headquarters of the regiment, the band, seven companies of troops numbering 450 officers and men and 60 supply wagons. The dragoons set off on horseback through Texas, leaving on July 25 and arriving at Corpus Christi on August 27, marching a total of 501.5 miles. The regiment "encountered difficulties on the route, and obstacles that seemed insurmountable; but nothing impeded our progress." They endured many hardships,

> *passing through a comparatively unsettled country, a Southern climate, a six weeks drought, the month of August, the various and contradictory reports in reference to forage, &c., with seven companies of Dragoons and a train of sixty wagons, might well have staggered a firmer and more practical mind. But the task, voluntarily undertaken, has been accomplished; and the regiment and train of wagons presented to the commanding General in such fine condition as to have elicited the admiration of our friend of the Infantry Regiments, and a complimentary order from General Taylor himself.*[150]

To avoid the extreme heat, the column would begin their march at three o'clock in the morning, march twenty-five to thirty miles, then set up camp around twelve o'clock. The soldiers often had to dismount and walk their horses to prevent the "miserable saddle lately adopted by the Government" from damaging the backs of their mounts. Despite the hardships of the march, there were only three deaths. One was on the first day, when a trooper overheated then drank too much cold water; the other two died from "a stroke of the sun" while walking their horses.[151]

The regiment had been ordered to rendezvous with General Taylor at San Patricio, north of Corpus Christi. To cross the Nueces River, a team of dragoons had been sent ahead to prepare rafts to transport supplies. The main body of troops started crossing at midnight, and by eight o'clock in the morning, all the troops had swum the river with their horses. The troops were now in disputed territory, and tensions were running high. During the crossing, the dragoons heard "what was at first supposed to be the firing of a salute at Corpus Christi. The continuation of the distant reports, however, together with the absence of Gen. Taylor," led the troops to fear that Corpus Christi was under attack. Twiggs prepared the regiment to ride to the rescue of the army. He assigned the sick and convalescents to remain and guard the supplies, while the rest of the command was ordered to mount their horses and form up. As the column was riding out, the officer in charge of the supply train reported that there were no sick to guard the wagons; all fifty had rejoined their companies for the attack. The force had advanced three miles when they saw riders coming up the road to meet them. Instead of being the forward troops of the Mexican Army, it was General Taylor, and the dragoons soon discovered that they were about to meet not a Mexican advance but "a violent thunderstorm." The regiment was "not much vexed, as the occurrence displayed to us the alacrity with which our men would prepare to meet the enemy, and the stuff the Regiment is made of. *Nous Verrons.*"[152]

Rumors were running wild in the United States about the condition of the dragoons on the march; there was even a report that Colonel Twiggs, "who had preceded the command an hour or two, was laying dangerously ill five miles on the road." To correct the erroneous reports, the officers of regiment wrote a letter to the editors of the *Picayune* "for the purpose of correcting the various rumors and reports in circulation." The officers reported that Twiggs was not ill, and in fact, "our gallant Colonel never flagged or wavered, notwithstanding a slight affliction at the commencement of the march; but conducted the command to this point with a rapidity, energy and masterly ability, in the highest degree creditable." Aside from the three deaths, the regiment was in good health, "in a thorough state of discipline, and full of alacrity to meet the enemy."[153]

With the departure of the dragoons, Lieutenant Inge was not only left in command of the garrison, but he was also serving as quartermaster and commissary and was the only commissioned officer on the post. On December 2, 1845, Lieutenant Inge received word that he was to move his command, along with surgeon Barnes and all the animals and other movable public property, overland to Austin, Texas, then proceed to join Taylor at Corpus Christi. The soldiers who were too sick to march overland were to be sent to New Orleans Barracks to recover. Inge was to begin his march as soon as an officer from the quartermaster's office arrived to oversee the remaining public property. Inge was ordered to sell the remaining supplies and items in the quartermaster's department at the fort that could not be taken with him or transported back to the department due to cost or condition.[154] With this, the military role of Fort Jesup came to an end. However, not only would war visit the site again, but the officers and soldiers who had lived and trained at Fort Jesup would also go on to shape American history for the next four decades.

CHAPTER 9

THE CIVIL WAR, WORLD WAR II AND EFFORTS TO SAVE THE FORGOTTEN FORT

With the conclusion of the Mexican-American War, Fort Jesup's military role came to an end, but the community that had grown up around the fort would continue. The buildings were destined to continue to serve new missions—some as homes, some as barns and some to educate the minds of a generation of young men. Just shy of one hundred years after Fort Jesup closed as a military post, it would be called on one more time to serve its country. It was occupied by part of Patton's army during the Great Louisiana Maneuvers, and the lessons learned in the pine woods of Louisiana and Texas would help save countless lives in the European Theater of World War II.

Once the soldiers left, Fort Jesup became a farming community. The reservation was divided into lots, and the first group was sold in April 1850. The fort's buildings were either converted to homes or torn down and the materials used to build homes and barns. The population grew slowly but steadily, and by the beginning of the twentieth century, the community of Fort Jesup was the largest town in Sabine Parish, even larger than the parish seat of government located in the town of Many. When Fort Jesup was founded in 1822, it was in Natchitoches Parish, but as the population of the former No Man's Land grew, Natchitoches Parish was divided into several new parishes, including Sabine Parish in 1843. Fort Jesup was considered as the parish seat, but the site was not centrally located and was still an active military post, so it was decided to create a town in the center of the parish at the crossroads of the Texas Road and the Alexandria

Road, centered on Baldwin's store. Baldwin had run a successful store and inn at the crossroads since the 1820s. Lands were divided into lots, and roads were laid out for the new town of Many, named after James B. Many, former commander at Fort Jesup.[155]

The quiet of peaceful farming community would be broken in 1864 when the Civil War came to western Louisiana during the Red River Campaign. A large Union army was sent into western Louisiana to capture Shreveport (the Confederate state capital after the fall of New Orleans and Baton Rouge) and then march into Texas, cutting off the Confederates' last major supply line. During the campaign, Walker's and Mouton's Divisions of the Confederate army camped at Fort Jesup on March 30, 1864. One soldier recalled that the barracks, sutler's store, commanding officer's quarters and several small houses were still standing, but they were in a state of decay. A few weeks later, these troops would take part in the Battle of Mansfield, which was the last major Confederate victory of the war and, the next day, the Battle of Pleasant Hill, which was the largest battle fought west of the Mississippi River.[156]

The first attempt to open a school at Fort Jesup after the military occupation took place in 1852 when a joint resolution of the Louisiana legislature asked for a donation of part of the military reservation of Fort Jesup to establish a "public seminary of education," but nothing came of the motion, as there was no president for the transfer of federal land to a state for educational purposes. Over the next forty years, the community of Fort Jesup continued to grow, and even though it was not the parish seat, it was the largest community in the parish and a major Masonic center. In 1886,

Annual reenactment of the Battle of Pleasant Hill. *Author's collection.*

Sabine Parish Lodge No. 75 decided to establish a college at Fort Jesup to bring the benefits of higher education to the community and to educate the children of deceased Master Masons. The Sabine High School Society was officially chartered on May 5, 1887, and work began on constructing school buildings and hiring faculty. Professor Thomas Rollins Hardin was selected as the head of the school. The school was named the Fort Jesup Masonic Institute and would eventually offer elementary, high school and college classes and boarding facilities. In 1889, the institute had three faculty members and eighty-three pupils and was described as follows:

The schoolhouse is built near the site of the Masonic Lodge…and is a commodious one story building some fifty feet in length by thirty-five to forty feet in width—a large room for recitation and study. It is furnished with newest shaped desks and benches with long series of black-board walls extending on both sides from one extreme end to the other, a large stove in the very center speaking volumes of the consideration of the projectors that the young attendants should be surrounded by every comfort in the winter, and the many windows giving in the light and cool breezes to prevent every discomfort arising from close rooms in the heated summer. To the left of the school building, some 20 yards distant, and to the right of the place where was at one time the residence of General Taylor, afterwards President of the United States, is a large two story structure, the sleeping apartments for the boarders of the Institute, dining room, parlor and other rooms.[157]

In his 1889 report of the board of directors to the people of Sabine Parish, the board's president, J.F. Smith, wrote:

The most approved methods of tuition have been adopted. The ancient languages and mathematics receive all necessary attention, and such prominence is given to the higher English and modern languages, as is demanded by the broader culture of the age. Discipline has been rigid, but certainly parental and kind. The departments are preparatory, academic and collegiate. Tuition for a term of twenty weeks, or a half session, in the preparatory department, is $10.00. In the academic department, $17.50. In the collegiate department, $25.00. Incidental fee, $1.00. This, however, does not include art lessons and music, which are extra. The president has charge of the advanced classes, and exercises a close supervision over all the departments, including the boarding department, which at the present time is in charge of our own worthy fellow citizen, Mr. W. P. Reed and his most

excellent and estimable lady. Board is furnished in the college at $8.00 per
month and may be had at the same price with any of the private families in
their comfortable homes in Fort Jesup or its vicinity.[158]

The student's day was filled with activities and studies, starting with the morning bell at 6:00 a.m. Breakfast was served at 7:00 a.m., and classroom instruction began at 8:00 a.m. and lasted until 12:10 p.m. After lunch, students had another block of classroom instruction from 1:00 p.m. until 3:30 p.m. Students would then spend time doing "physical exercises" (both indoor and outdoor) until 6:00 p.m. Supper was served at 6:10 p.m., with a study hall from 7:30 to 10:00 pm. All lights were to be extinguished at 10:30. It was expected that students boarding in the community would keep the early morning and evening schedule as closely as possible. On average, the school year began September 10 and continued until June 14, with only two days off: one day for Thanksgiving and one day for Christmas.[159]

One feature of the school that was heavily advertised was the overall healthiness of the location; the school claimed to be "Located at One of the Most Healthful Points in the Highlands of West Louisiana." The advertisements were often accompanied by endorsements from local doctors; one such was an 1894 publication that quoted Dr. J.C. "Crit" Armstrong of Many: "I have practiced medicine in Fort Jesup and vicinity for 43 years. I know of no place in the country so remarkable for the health of its people. I have never known of a single case of malarial trouble occurring there. It gives me great pleasure to observe that an institution of learning of so great promise is being built in [our] midst."[160]

The completion of the first academic year of the Institute on June 7, 1889, was a time for celebration for the entire community:

Long before the appointed hour 8 a.m., the beginning hour for the exercises
at the Fort Jesup Masonic Institute, the roads leading thereto were alive
with vehicles, and the footpaths gay with the pupils in white dresses and
many colored ribbons and such visitors as lived within walking distance
of the buildings and grounds. Booths had already been erected, one at the
entrance and another to the right of it and further back, displaying from their
rough made shelves, wares tempting to hungry and thirsty alike. Tables, long
and narrow, of rough dressed pine boards were arranged under the largest
and shadiest trees, and in the bustling school room could be discerned that
preparations were still going on to give the greatest comfort and enjoyment to
the concourse to be entertained during the day.[161]

The Fort Jesup Masonic Institute continued to grow for several more years, but the institute was founded at a time when private institutions of education were on the decline, as interest grew in public education and the creation of parish school boards instead of private schools. The early schools in Sabine Parish were under the jurisdiction of the police jury (parish government), but by 1871, a parish school board separate from the police jury had been created; it held its first official meeting on August 1, 1871. In 1890, the Sabine Parish School Board entered into agreement with the Fort Jesup Masonic Institute to open a public school in connection with the institute. Also, in 1890, the Louisiana legislature awarded the Masonic Institute the authority to confer degrees and diplomas in letters and arts "known to universities and colleges in Europe and America."[162]

By 1894, increased opportunities for public schools and improved transportation led to a decline in private school and boarding school attendance, and the Fort Jesup Masonic Institute was no exception. Attendance at the institute began to decline, and by January 1896, a committee from the institute began working with the Sabine Parish School Board to donate the unencumbered buildings and property to the school board. By July, all the legal arrangements had been completed for the transfer of the property, and plans were made for the opening of Central High School for the 1896–97 school year. Central would be the first public high school in the parish, with an enrollment of 153 pupils the first year. Instead of the nine-month term the institute had, all public schools in Sabine Parish had three-month terms, which for Central would start on October 5, 1896. Tuition for the school was one dollar per month, with incidental fees not to exceed seventy-five cents for the term. Boarding was still available for between six and eight dollars per month.

With the arrival of the Kansas City Southern Railroad in 1896, Sabine Parish saw the beginning of an economic boom that would last for several decades, but the decision to run the railroad through the parish seat of Many ended the growth and prosperity of the community of Fort Jesup, which started a steady decline as more and more businesses and citizens moved to Many to be closer to the railroad. When a fire destroyed the main school buildings of Central High School in 1907, it was decided to move the high school to Many instead of rebuilding. An elementary school would continue at Fort Jesup until 1917, but eventually, it was closed as well. The decline of Fort Jesup was summed up in 1939 in a speech by Eddie Stoker at the dedication of the Pendleton-Gaines Memorial Bridge across the Sabine River: "It may not be generally known that at one time

Fort Jesup boasted of a hotel, a printing shop, newspaper, drug store, five general stores, a college, Woodman Hall, and one of the oldest Masonic Lodges int the state, Sabine 75."[163]

As the community faded, so did the memory of the old fort, and by the time Central High School closed in 1907, most of the fort's buildings had either rotted away or been torn down and their materials used for houses and barns in the community. Only one of the enlisted men's kitchens/mess halls remained, and it was in danger of collapse. The roof and floor were gone, and the stone foundation was so weak it could barely hold the weight of the building. Although many of the hundred-year-old timbers had rotted, enough of them were intact to allow the building to be preserved, but the clock was ticking, and no one seemed to be able to organize the type of group needed to save the building.

The site of the old fort had become a popular picnic and meeting ground, and that fact helped to keep at least the location of the old post and the condition of the remaining building in the minds of the community. From time to time, there would be interest in the preservation of the ruins, but the effort would die from lack of leadership. Beginning in the late 1920s, several of the ladies' service clubs of Many began to work together to preserve the site, with the Athena Delphian Club taking the lead. Their first act was to place a bronze historical marker near the site with historical information and to honor the work of Professor Thomas Rollins Hardin and his wife, Sarah Fair Hardin, for their roles in the history of the Fort Jesup Masonic Institute. The tablet is still standing, although it was moved to a new location in the 1960s.[164]

Next, the committee of women from Many began working to raise money and attempted to secure federal aid for the preservation. The committee was made up of Mrs. W.M. Knott, Mrs. I.L. Pace, Mrs. R. Pattison, Mrs. O.B. Williams, Mrs. E.M. Fraser, Mrs. Alice Nash, Mrs. J.D. Williams, Mrs. H.H. Kennedy, Mrs. G.C. Reeves (chairwoman) and Mrs. S.D. Ponder, assisted by Congressman James B. Aswell. Under the Act of June 11, 1926, which was "to provide for the study and investigation of battlefields in the United States or other adjacent points of historic or military interest for commemorative purposes," Congressman Aswell was able to work with the secretary of war, who ordered Colonel H.L. Landers of the Historical Section of the Army War College to conduct an inspection in December 1929. Colonel Landers gave a favorable recommendation for the preservation of the site, and the secretary of war recommend the erection of a marker on the site by the federal government at a cost of $5,000. The recommendation was

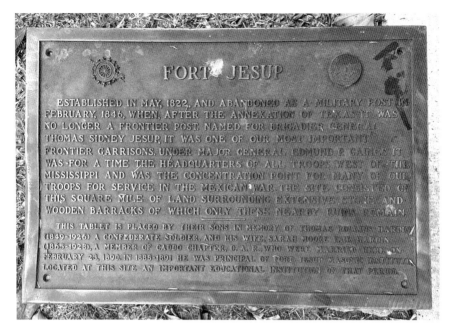

The first historical marker for Fort Jesup, now located on the grounds of Fort Jesup State Historic Site. *Photo by author.*

introduced by Congressman Aswell as House Bill No. 8873, Seventy-Second U.S. Congress, on January 22, 1930, but the bill was defeated in committee.[165]

This defeat did not stop the preservation work, and soon, the family of the late P.E. Well, who had been a Sabine Parish Police Jury member, and Philip A Koonce, Homer Koonce and Mrs. Charles Koonce Matlock presented "deeds of donation" to the Sabine Parish Police Jury for "lots 20 and 21 of the subdivision of the south half of section 4, township 7 north, range 10 west, Sabine Parish which contained the log kitchen and remaining stone pillars of the barracks that had been in front of the kitchen. Along with the donation of land was also $800.00 for the restoration of the building which was later raised to $1,100.00 (roughly $16,161.19 in 2022) as more donations were added to it to finish the preservation work and build a decorative fence around the land. The work was overseen by architects Tudor and Ratcliff of Alexandria, who were also building the Methodist church in Many, and construction was carried out by John R. Fisher. The work included replacing the roof with hand-riven cypress boards; rebuilding the old rock chimney; replacing decayed logs with sound, hewn logs in walls; restoring sills where needed; using original hand-wrought hinges on doors and windows; fashioning wooden latches; providing a new floor of rough oak boards; and replacing the stone foundation. Also, at this time, it was discovered by R.A. Fraser and Gasway German that lot 22, roughly .44 acres, had never been sold by the government. This land was added to the park, which now contained about three acres. Prisoners were used in clearing the land, hauling materials and building the fence, under the supervision of the parish agricultural agent, E.F. Fletcher. A Mr. Wells had also donated a widened right of way along the road leading from Highway 6 to the park, and the state highway commission restored the road to good condition. After the preservation work was completed, the committee continued to plant trees and shrubs and maintain the grounds. The site soon became a favorite of religious and civic groups for outdoor meetings and picnics.[166]

The quiet of Fort Jesup would again be broken with the rise of Adolf Hitler and Nazi Germany, and soon, American troops would use Fort Jesup as a training ground again. Realizing that their tactics and equipment could not stand up to the German Blitz, the War Department planned the largest war games in U.S. history. On the first day of what became known as the Great Maneuvers (September 15, 1941), General Patton pushed his Red Army armored units across the Red River near Montgomery, Louisiana, and by the afternoon began attacking advanced units of the Blue Army at Fort Jesup. Patton's tanks pushed the mounted troops of the First Cavalry Division out of their positions and drove them down the road toward Many. During the battle, one of Patton's tanks ran over the historical marker near the highway, which still bears a scar from the encounter. By that evening, the Red Army had established a twenty-mile front from Fort Jesup to the Sabine River. On September 18, Blue forces launched harassing attacks on Fort Jesup but did not launch a full-scale attack on the old fort. The failure of the Red Army to halt the Blue Army at several other key points led to the withdraw of the Red Army from Fort Jesup, and on September 20, the first phase of the maneuvers was completed, with the Blue Army declared the winner. The tanks rolled out, but within a few months, the United States found itself in World War II. Lessons learned in the Great Maneuvers about how to use tanks in combat, what type of formations to use and the integration of new technologies would play a key role in the Allied victory. Officers who had proven themselves in the war games, such as Patton and Eisenhower, were quickly promoted as several unsuccessful officers were retired.[167]

Not only would World War II be the last time that Fort Jesup was used for military purposes, but the war years would also be detrimental to the preservation of the historic site. As more young men went to war, it became harder and harder to find people to take care of the grounds, and the community's energy was directed toward the war effort, even to the point where the iron fence around the park was donated to the scrap-iron drive. It was not until 1951 that there was a major push to continue the preservation efforts.[168]

The first effort to have Fort Jesup become a state park was in 1951, when it was suggested that the site could be used as a highway wayside park. However, the State Parks and Recreation Commission felt that "its location on Highway No. 6, which is not a major state highway, would not justify the expense of the project." Next, the community turned to the National Park Service for help, led by Judge William Ponder, who began corresponding with Congressman George S. Long about the possibility of having Fort Jesup become a National Historic Site. Judge Ponder began researching the history of the site and writing to Congressman Long in 1953. Long shared the research with the Legislative Reference Service of the Library of Congress and asked for them to review the information and advise him on the best course of action. Both the Library of Congress and the director of the National Park Service felt that the site's historical significance warranted consideration for the creation of a national park; the issue was the amount of land available. At that time, the requirement for land to create a national park was a minimum of twenty acres. Conrad L. Wirth, director of the National Park Service, wrote to Long on March 25, 1954, informing him that the lack of land would probably result in a negative recommendation from the advisory board, and he suggested that the committee try to get the state to preserve the site. Long communicated this to Judge Ponder and suggested that if the committee could convince the state government to purchase more land, fence it and make some improvements, Long would resubmit the proposal to the National Park Service. With the ball put back in the community's court, Judge Ponder and Mrs. W.M. Knott set to work. Mrs. W.M. Knott had been involved with the preservation effort since the beginning and had assisted Judge Ponder with correspondence and research; now, she set to work trying to get community support. Mrs. Knott introduced a resolution at the state board meeting of the Daughters of the American Revolution in October 1954, requesting that the State of Louisiana create a historical park at Fort Jesup and provide funds to purchase additional lands, restore the site and preserve and maintain the park. Similar resolutions were passed in March and April 1955 by the Sabine Parish School Board, Sabine Parish Police Jury and the Floyd Jordon Post of the American Legion, urging support for the park from the legislature. On May 6, House Bill No. 7 Act No. 133 was submitted in the fiscal session by J.M. Belisle, representative from

Sabine Parish. Much of the language of the bill had been written by Judge Ponder. The bill called for the State Parks and Recreation Commission to be authorized to acquire land by "donation or purchase or any other manner of acquisition" for the purpose of preserving of Old Fort Jesup, and a sum of $75,000 was requested from the general fund for the "development and maintenance and upkeep" of the park. The bill was killed in committee.[169]

Instead of giving up, the concerned citizens redoubled their efforts. Each organization passed another resolution stating its support for the Fort Jesup Park, and the Daughters of the American Revolution added to their resolution that "the structure be restored as a Zachary Taylor Memorial." Community members and elected officials were contacted by letter and in person to increase interest in the preservation of the site. Belisle reintroduced the bill, this time in the regular session, and the bill was passed quickly by the House of Representatives and the Senate in June 1956 and signed by Governor Earl K. Long (Mrs. Knott's brother) on July 3, 1956. With that, work began to plan and construct the Fort Jesup Park and Museum. The year 1957 was spent acquiring the land for the park, mostly throughs donation, which, in the end, would total around twenty-two acres: twenty acres for the park and two acres across the road, which was used for the manager's residence and maintenance facilities. The development team decided that they would select one of the officers' quarters that was originally on the eastern side of the parade ground to rebuild to house the museum, even though it would not be on the original site. The building was selected because "it was most commodious to our needs for a meeting hall, information center, with a third floor for future museum expansion." Clay Watson, the museum technician for the Louisiana State Parks Commission, wrote near the end of the reconstruction that "in the museum is told the story of this military outpost with the use of maps, documents, and illustrations. A diorama will show the fort under reconstruction in the 1830s. Military artifacts of the period will round out the collection." The Department of Public Works and State Highway Commission aided the State Parks and Recreation Commission by installing water and sewage pipes and building the road. The concept was that the picnic area would be used as a roadside rest area and would be open for use, there would be a modest fee to tour the museum and the first floor would be a meeting room/reunion hall, which could be rented for a fee.[170]

The park was dedicated at two o'clock on Sunday, March 27, 1960, with a military gun salute and flag-raising ceremony by the Louisiana National Guard and Floyd Jordan Post of the American Legion. The dedication program lasted about an hour, with speeches by A.A. Fredericks, executive

Program from the dedication of the Fort Jesup Park. *Courtesy of the Louisiana Office of State Parks, Fort Jesup State Historic Site.*

Picture of the dedication of the Fort Jesup Park. *Courtesy of the Louisiana Office of State Parks, Fort Jesup State Historic Site..*

secretary to Governor Earl K. Long, and district attorney J. Reuel Boone, who gave the welcoming address and acted as master of ceremonies in the absence of Senator F.E. Cole, who was ill. Judge William H. Ponder, who had been one of the driving forces behind the Fort Jesup project, gave the historical address, which focused on "the greatness of the men whose lives and destinies had been entwined throughout the history of Fort Jesup" and how present and future generations should aspire to greatness in "our lives and deeds."[171]

Over the next fifty or so years, the park continued to serve the public as thousands of visitors traveled to the site for tours, family reunions and civic functions. In the 1990s, a living history program was started, in which tour guides and volunteers would dress in accurate reproductions of uniforms and clothing to help educate the public about daily life at the fort. The museum has been updated several times since its opening, and in the 1990s, it was expanded to include the first floor, as well. Thousands of schoolchildren have toured the site on school field trips since 1960, helping history thrive as more than words in old textbooks.

Dorothie Erwin of the *Shreveport Times* wrote on the eve of the dedication that "old Army Posts, like old soldiers, do die. Abandoned and neglected, they fade away until the reality of men and missions and buildings recedes and becomes only a colorless name in a dusty historical tome. They do, that is, unless the last few vestiges of reality are rescued from the edge of oblivion, and then carefully refurbished and thoughtfully preserved."[172] Had a group of concerned citizens not stepped up to save Fort Jesup, it would have been lost to time, but their generation has passed into history, and new threats from statewide economic challenges, changing patterns of visitation, high costs of events and exhibits and time itself now threaten the site. The Louisiana Office of State Parks is committed to preserving the physical remains of the site but cannot do it alone. Without active educational programs for visitors, youth and community members to teach them about the site, future generations will not be able to learn about the important historical and cultural events that took place at this fort and the stories that it and other historic sites have to tell, and soon they will be lost to history, the remains nothing more than empty buildings with no meaning. However, unwilling to allow their beloved Fort Jesup to fade away, a new generation of concerned citizens is working with the Office of State Parks to help preserve the site and tell the important stories of the men and women who called Fort Jesup home and the effect they had on American history. They have formed the Friends of Fort Jesup Historic

Site, a 501(c)(3) nonprofit group dedicated to hosting living history events at the site and raising money through fundraisers, donations and grants to help improve and maintain the site. Only the future knows what will happen to old Fort Jesup, but if we all band together, the old army post will have another two hundred or more years, and the stories of the soldiers who served our country will not fade away.

NOTES

Chapter 1

1. The previous paragraphs are a short summary of the Neutral Strip. For a more detailed explanation, see the following: Marshall, *Western Boundary*; Leckie, *From Sea to Shining Sea*; Linklater, *Artist in Treason*, 8; and Fredriksen, *Military Leaders*.
2. Marshall, *Western Boundary*, 239–41.
3. Johnson, "Seventh Regiment of Infantry"; McManus, *American Courage*, 35–36.
4. McManus, *American Courage*, 35–36.
5. Gray, *Old Soldier's Story*, 39.
6. Heitman, *Historical Register and Dictionary*, 219; McManus, *American Courage*, 38–39.
7. Birch, *Journal*, 123.
8. Gray, *Old Soldier's Story*, 41.
9. Ibid., 42.
10. Fredriksen, *Military Leaders*, 798–99, Leckie, *From Sea to Shining Sea*, 510–15.
11. Birch, *Journal*, 125.
12. Gray, *Old Soldier's Story*, 42–43, Birch, *Journal*, 125.
13. Gray, *Old Soldier's Story*, 43.
14. Ibid., 44, Birch, *Journal*, 126–27, 130.
15. Thompson, *Confederate General of the West*, 9.
16. Gray, *Old Soldier's Story*, 44.
17. Middleton, "Frontier Outpost," 47–49.

18. Gray, *Old Soldier's Story*, 44.

19. Ibid., 44–45.

20. Thompson, *Confederate General*, 10.

21. Birch, *Journal*, 131.

22. Ibid., 132; Hardin, *Fort Jesup*, 16.

23. Hardin, *Fort Jesup*, 11.

24. *Fort Jesup Historic Collection* Book M, 3. Hereafter referred to as FJHC.

25. Hardin, *Fort Jesup*, 11–12.

26. Middleton, "Frontier Outpost," 54–55.

27. Birch, *Journal*, 134–35.

28. Ibid., 135.

Chapter 2

29. Bauer, *Zachary Taylor*, 33, 41.

30. Frazer, *Forts of the West*, xxi.

31. Middleton, "Frontier Outpost," 54.

32. Lawson, *Statistical Report*, 237.

33. Gray, *Old Soldier's Story*, 48.

34. FJHC Book 1, 9; Gray, *Old Soldier's Story*, 48.

35. Gray, *Old Soldier's Story*, 46–47.

36. Ibid., 47–48.

37. FJHC Book 3, 5; Middleton, "Frontier Outpost," 56.

38. Katcher, *Mexican American War*, 5.

39. Winders, *Mr. Polk's Army*, 17–21; Prucha, *Army Life*, 103, 105.

40. Moore and Haynes, *Tailor Made*, 33–35.

41. W. Brown, *Called It Home*, 71.

42. Elting, *American Army Life*, 59; Prucha, *Army Life*, 63–64.

43. Lawson, *Statistical Report*, 238; Elting, *American Army Life*, 61.

44. For a detailed social history study of the officers, women, children and enlisted soldiers, see Coffman, *Old Army*.

45. Winders, *Mr. Polk's Army*, 22.

46. Middleton, "Frontier Outpost," 65; Winters, *Mr. Polk's Army*, 89; Casey, *Encyclopedia*, 95.

47. Casey, *Encyclopedia*, 1–2; FJHC, Book 1, 5.

48. FJHC, Book 1, 12; Casey, *Encyclopedia*, 94.

49. FJHC, Book 1, 14–16, 34–37, 17–19.

Chapter 3

50. Hardin, *Fort Jesup*, 15.
51. Norris, personal communication; Richardson, Wallace and Anderson, *Lone Star State*, 66.
52. Gray, *Old Soldier's Story*, 49.
53. Middleton, "Frontier Outpost," 113–17.
54. Gray, *Old Soldier's Story*, 49–50.
55. Brands, *Lone Star Nation*, 106–9, Richardson, Wallace and Anderson, *Lone Star State*, 71.
56. Gray, *Old Soldier's Story*, p 50-56, Richardson, Wallace and Anderson, *Lone Star State*, 71.
57. Hardin, *Fort Jesup*, 16.
58. Ibid., 17–20; Middleton, "Frontier Outpost," 122–24; Ferris, *Founders and Frontiersmen*, 199; Gray, *Old Soldier's Story*, 56.
59. Gray, *Old Soldier's Story*, 57–58.
60. Ibid., 58–60.
61. FJHC, Book 2, 55.

Chapter 4

62. McRare, "Third Regiment of Infantry," 432–34.
63. Fredriksen, *Military Leaders*, 417–18; Barbuto, "Henry Leavenworth."
64. FJHC, Book 2, 65–66.
65. Ibid., 65–66, 69; FJHC, Book M, 27.
66. FJHC, Book 3, 1, 3–4; Casey, *Encyclopedia*, 5–6.
67. Frazer, *Forts of the West*, xxi; FJHC Book 3, 7.
68. FJHC, Book 3, 46; Jackson, *Almonte's Texas*, 95; FJHC, Book 3, 49.
69. Urwin, *United States Cavalry*, 61–62.
70. Homas, "Latc Gen. Leavenworth," 108; Casey, *Encyclopedia*, 95.
71. FJHC, Book 3, 58–59.
72. Girard, *Caddos and Their Ancestors*, 107–11; Brock, "Caddo Indian Treaty."
73. FJHC, Book 3, 67; Hardin, *Fort Jesup*, 23–25; Girard, *Caddos and Their Ancestors*, 107; Graham, "Bonnell, Joseph."
74. Girard, *Caddos and Their Ancestors*, 111.

Chapter 5

75. For a detailed study of the prewar years in Texas, see Brands, *Lone Star Nation*.
76. Davis, *Three Roads*, 227.

77. Ibid., 227–32.
78. Ibid., 259.
79. Brands, *Lone Star Nation*, 162–63.
80. Anderson, *Conquest of Texas*, 72; FJHC, Book 3, 8.
81. Jackson, *Almonte's Texas*, 93.
82. Haythornthwaite, *Alamo*, 6.
83. Walraven and Walraven, *Magnificent Barbarians*, 116.
84. Graham, "Bonnell, Joseph."
85. Brands, *Lone Star Nation*, 293; Walraven and Walraven, *Magnificent Barbarians*, 187–200, Haythornthwaite, *Alamo*, 11–15.
86. Marshall, *Western Boundary*, 148.
87. Ibid., 152.
88. Ibid., 156–57.
89. Graham, "Bonnell, Joseph."
90. Haythornthwaite, *Alamo*, 19–22.
91. Walraven and Walraven, *Magnificent Barbarians*, 103, 112–14.
92. Ibid., 114–15.
93. Ibid., 117–18.
94. Ibid., 118.
95. Ibid., 118–19.

Chapter 6

96. For a detailed study of the Seminole Wars, see Missall and Missall, *Seminole Wars*.
97. FJHC, Book 3, 94, 99.
98. Ibid., 94, 99.
99. Ibid., 94–100.
100. Ibid., 104, 107–8.
101. Ehrlich, *They Have No Rights*, 11, 22, 23.
102. FJHC, Book 3, 99; Rodriguez, "Complicity and Deceit," 139–47.
103. FJHC, Book 3, 110.
104. *Army and Navy Chronicle*, "Correspondence of the Army and Navy Chronicle," 41, 58, 56.
105. *Army and Navy Chronicle*, "Fort Jesup," 5.
106. *Army and Navy Chronicle* 9, no. 11: 167.
107. FJHC, Book 4, 7–8; Urwin, *United States Infantry*, 57–58.
108. Urwin, *United States Infantry*, 57–58; Seminole Nation Museum, "Seminole Wars."
109. Jarvis, letter to Will, March 25, 1844.

Chapter 7

110. Urwin, *Cavalry*, 58.
111. Thompson, *Confederate General*, 10, 23, 25, 42.
112. R. Brown, "Old Woman," 58.
113. FJHC, Book 4, 13.
114. Ibid., 14–15, 18.
115. Jarvis, letter to Will, March 31, 1842.
116. Rodenbough, *From Everglade to Canyon*, 83–84.
117. FJHC, Book 4, 1, 25, 29, 37; FJHC, Book M, 41, 43.
118. Ibid., 36, 48.
119. Ibid., 25, 27.
120. Langellier, *US Dragoons 1833–55*, 18.
121. FJHC, Book 4, 36, 38; Jarvis, letter to Will, May 23, 1843.
122. Ibid., 34–35, 40.
123. Jarvis, letter to Will, May 23, 1843.
124. Rodenbough, *From Everglade to Canyon*, 83.
125. Prucha, *Army Life*, 131.
126. Ibid.; Jarvis, letter to Will, March 31, 1842.
127. Jarvis, letter to Will, May 23, 1843.

Chapter 8

128. Bauer, *Zachary Taylor*, 111–12.
129. Rodenbough, *From Everglade to Canyon*, 85–86.
130. Croffut, *Fifty Years*, 185.
131. Ibid.
132. Grant, *Memoirs*, 48–51.
133. Ibid., 52–53; Perret, *Grant*, 44–45.
134. Grant, *Memoirs*, 56; Perret, *Grant*, 45.
135. Goetzmann, "First Foreign War."
136. Katcher, *Mexican Americam War*, 3; Croffut, *Fifty Years*, 185; FJHC, Book M, 59.
137. Bauer, *Zachary Taylor*, 113.
138. Ibid.
139. FJHC, Book 4, 58.
140. Ibid., 60–61.
141. Bauer, *Zachary Taylor*, 113; Croffut, *Fifty Years*, 187.
142. Croffut, *Fifty Years*, 187–88.
143. Perret, *Grant*, 47.

144. Grant, *Memoirs*, 58.

145. Hardin, *Fort Jesup*, 66–67.

146. Croffut, *Fifty Years*, 189.

147. Bauer, *Zachary Taylor*, 115–16; Hardin, *Fort Jesup*, 65–66.

148. Croffut, *Fifty Years*, 191–92.

149. Goetzmann, "First Foreign War."

150. "More of the Movement of Our Troops," *Daily Picayune*.

151. "March of the 2nd Dragoons," *Daily Picayune*.

152. Ibid.

153. Ibid.

154. FJHC, Book 4, 65–67.

Chapter 9

155. Casey, *Encyclopedia*, 98; Clements, *Many, LA*, 13.

156. Casey, *Encyclopedia*, 99.

157. Hays, "Fort Jesup," 24–28.

158. Ibid. 29.

159. Clements, *Many, LA*, 58.

160. Ibid.

161. Hays, "Fort Jesup," 29.

162. Ibid., 30–31, Clements, *Many, LA*, 49.

163. Hays, "Fort Jesup," 31–32, Clements, *Many, LA*, 57.

164. Hays, "Fort Jesup," 34.

165. Ibid., 34–35.

166. Ibid., 35–38.

167. Gabel, *GHQ Maneuvers of 1941*, 70–86; Robertson, "General Patton."

168. Hays, "Fort Jesup," 38.

169. Ibid., 38–43.

170. Ibid., 43–47; Watson, "Louisiana's Newest State Park."

171. Hays, "Fort Jesup," 48–49.

172. Ibid., 49.

BIBLIOGRAPHY

Primary Sources

Army and Navy Chronicle 9, no. 11 (September 12, 1839).

Birch, George. *Journal and Family Papers*. N.d. Copy of the original in the Historical Society of Pennsylvania.

"Correspondence of the Army and Navy Chronicle." *Army and Navy Chronicle*, January 17, 1839.

"Fort Jesup." *Army and Navy Chronicle* 8, no. 1.

Fort Jesup Historic Collection. 5 vols. On file at Fort Jesup State Historic Site.

Grant, Ulysses. *Personal Memoirs*. 2 vols. Sampson, Law, Martion: 1885–86.

Gray, Charles Martin. *The Old Soldier's Story: Autobiography of Charles Martin Gray, Co. A, 7th Regiment, United States Infantry, Embracing Interesting and Exciting Incidents of the Army Life on the Frontier, in the Early Part of the Present Century*. Edgefield, SC: Edgefield Advertiser Print, 1868. Copied from the collections in the Center for American History, University of Texas at Austin.

Heitman, Francis Bernard. *Historical Register and Dictionary of the United States Army: From Its Organization, September 29, 1789, to March 2, 1903*. Vol. 1. Washington D.C.: U.S. Government Printing Office, 1903.

Homas, Benjamin, ed. "The Late Gen. Leavenworth." *Army and Navy Chronicle* 1, no. 10 (March 5, 1835).

Jarvis, N.S. Letters of N.S. Jarvis. Collection in the New York Academy of Medicine Library, New York, NY.

Lawson, Thomas. *Statistical Report on the Sickness and Mortality of the Army of the United States.* 1840.

Published Sources

Anderson, Gary Clayton. *The Conquest of Texas.* Norman: University of Oklahoma Press, 2005.

Bauer, K. Jack, *Zachary Taylor: Soldier, Planter, Statesman of the Old Southwest.* Baton Rouge: Louisiana State University Press, 1985.

Brands, H.W. *Lone Star Nation.* New York: Doubleday, 2004.

Brown, Russell K. "An Old Woman with a Broomstick: General David E. Twiggs and the U.S. Surrender in Texas, 1861." *Military Affairs* 48, no. 2 (April 1984).

Brown, William L., III. *The Army Called It Home: Military Interiors of the 19th Century.* Gettysburg, PA: Thomas Publications, 1992.

Casey, Powell. *Encyclopedia of Forts, Posts, Named Camps, and Other Military Installations in Louisiana, 1700–1981.* Baton Rouge, LA: Claitor's Publishing, 1983.

Clements, Shannon. *Many, LA: Reflections of Our Town.* Many, LA: Sweet Dreams Publishing Company, 1999.

Coffman, Edward M. *The Old Army: A Portrait of the American Army in Peacetime 1784–1898.* New York: Oxford University Press, 1986.

Croffut, W.A., ed. *Fifty Years in Camp and Field.* New York: G. P. Putnam's Sons, 1909.

Davis, William C. *Three Roads to the Alamo.* New York: Harper Perennial, 1998.

Ehrlich, Walter. *They Have No Rights: Dred Scott's Struggle for Freedom.* Bedford, MA: Applewood Books, 1979.

Elting, John R. *American Army Life.* New York: Charles Scribner's Sons, 1982.

Ferris, Robert G. *Founders and Frontiersmen.* Washington, D.C.: United States Department of the Interior, National Park Service, 1967.

Frazer, Robert W. *Forts of the West: Military Forts and Presidios and Post Commonly Called Forts West of the Mississippi River to 1898.* Norman: University of Oklahoma Press, 1965.

Fredriksen, John C. *American Military Leaders from Colonial Times to Present.* Santa Barbara, CA:. ABC-CLIO, 1999.

Gabel, Christopher R. *The U.S. Army GHQ Maneuvers of 1941.* Washington, D.C.: Center of Military History, United States Army, 1992.

Girard, Jeffrey S. *The Caddos and Their Ancestors: Archaeology and the Native People of Northwest Louisiana.* Baton Rouge: Louisiana State University Press, 2018.

Goetzmann, William F. "Our First Foreign War." *American Heritage Magazine* 17, no. 4 (June 1966).

Hardin, J. Fair. *Fort Jesup—Fort Selden—Camp Sabine—Camp Salubrity: Four Forgotten Frontier Army Posts of Western Louisiana.* Metairie, LA: Louisiana Historical Society, 1933.

Hays, Elma B. "Fort Jesup from 1822–1960." Unpublished research report submitted to Northwestern State College, 1960.

Haythornthwaite, Philip. *The Alamo and the War of Texas Independence 1835–36.* Oxford: Osprey Press, 1999.

Heitman, Francis Bernard. *Historical Register and Dictionary of the United States Army: From Its Organization, September 29, 1789, to March 2, 1903.* Vol. 1. Washington, D.C.: U.S. Government Printing Office, 1903.

Jackson, Jack, ed. *Almonte's Texas.* Trans. John Wheat. Austin: Texas State Historical Association, 2003.

Johnson, A.B. "The Seventh Regiment of Infantry." In *The Army of the United States: Historical Sketches of Staff and Line with Portraits of Generals and Chiefs*, edited by Theophilus Francis Rodenbough and William L. Haskin. New York: Maynard, Merrill, 1896.

Katcher, Philip. *The Mexican American War, 1846–1848.* London: Osprey Press, 1992.

Langellier, John. *US Dragoons 1833–55.* Oxford: Osprey Press, 1995.

Leckie, Robert. *From Sea to Shining Sea: From the War of 1812 to the Mexican War, the Saga of America's Expansion.* New York: Harper Perennial, 1994.

Linklater, Andro. *An Artist in Treason: The Extraordinary Double Life of General James Wilkinson.* New York: Walker and Company, 2009.

Marshall, Thomas Maitland. *History of the Western Boundary of the Louisiana Purchase, 1819–1841.* Berkeley: University of California Press, 1914.

McManus, John C. *American Courage, American Carnage.* New York: Doherty Associates, 2009.

McRare, J. H. "The Third Regiment of Infantry." In *The Army of the United States: Historical Sketches of Staff and Line with Portraits of Generals-in-Chief*, edited by Theophilus F. Rodenbough. New York, NY: Maynard, Merrill, 1896.

Middleton, Harry F. "Frontier Outpost: A History of Fort Jesup, Louisiana." Master's thesis, Louisiana State University, 1973.

Missall, John, and Mary Lou Missall. *The Seminole Wars.* Gainsville: University Press of Florida, 2004.

Moore, Robert J., Jr., and Michael Haynes. *Tailor Made, Trail Worn: Army Life, Clothing and Weapons of the Corps of Discovery.* Helena, MT: Faircountry Press, 2003.

Perret, Geoffrey. *Ulysses S. Grant: Soldier and President.* New York: Modern Library, Random House, 1997.

Prucha, Francis Paul, ed. *Army Life on the Western Frontier.* Norman: University of Oklahoma Press, 1959.

Richardson, Rupert N., Ernest Wallace and Adrian N. Anderson. *Texas: The Lone Star State.* 3rd ed. Englewood Cliffs, NJ: Prentice-Hall, 1970.

Rodenbough, Theophilus F. *From Everglade to Canyon with the Second United States Cavalry: An Authentic Account of Service in Florida, Mexico, Virginia, and the Indian Country, 1836–1875.* New York: Van Nostrand, 1875. Repr., Norman: University of Oklahoma Press, 2000.

Rodriguez, Junius P. "Complicity and Deceit: Lewis Chaney's Plot and Its Bloody Consequences." In *Lethal Imagination: Violence and Brutality in American History*, edited by Michael A. Bellesiles. New York: New York University Press, 1999.

Thompson, Jerry, *Confederate General of the West, Henry Hopkins Sibley.* College Station: Texas A&M University Press, 1996.

Urwin, Gregory J.W. *The United States Cavalry: An Illustrated History 1776–1944.* Norman: University of Oklahoma Press, 2003.

———. *The United States Infantry: An Illustrated History 1775–1918.* Norman: University of Oklahoma Press, 1988.

Walraven, Bill, and Marjorie Walraven. *The Magnificent Barbarians.* Austin, TX: Eakin Press, 1993.

Watson, Clay. "Louisiana's Newest State Park." Copy from a public relations publication on file at Fort Jesup SHS.

Winders, Richard Bruce. *Mr. Polk's Army: The American Military Experience in the Mexican War.* College Station: Texas A&M University Press, 1997.

Online Resources

Barbuto, Rich. "Henry Leavenworth." Fort Leavenworth Historical Society.

Brock, Eric J. "The Caddo Indian Treaty." *64 Parishes* (October 11, 2020). https://64parishes.org/entry/the-caddo-indian-treaty#:~:text=The%20 Caddo%20Indian%20Treaty%20of,establishment%20of%20 present%2Dday%20Shreveport

Daily Picayune (New Orleans). "The March of the 2nd Dragoons." September 25, 1845.

———. "More of the Movement of Our Troops." N.d.

Graham, Seldon B., Jr. "Bonnell, Joseph." Handbook of Texas Online. Accessed March 15, 2022. https://www.tshaonline.org/handbook/entries/bonnell-joseph.

Miller, Ed. "The New Orleans Greys Uniform: A Historical Perspective." Sons of DeWitt Colony Texas. http://www.sonsofdewittcolony.org//adp/archives/feature/miller_greys/frameset.html.

Norris, Frank. Email to the author. June 11, 2015.

Robertson, Rickey. "General Patton in Louisiana 1941." Stephen F. Austin State University. Accessed June 20, 2016. https://www.sfasu.edu/heritagecenter/9633.asp.

Seminole Nation Museum. "The Seminole Wars." Accessed January 1, 2019. https://www.seminolenationmuseum.org.

Wettemann, Robert P., Jr. "'Jackson's Men' and Army Grey: Clothing the Volunteer Companies from New Orleans." Sons of DeWitt Colony Texas. http://www.sonsofdewittcolony.org//adp/archives/feature/wetterman.html#fn31.

ABOUT THE AUTHOR

Courtesy of David Maroski.

Scott DeBose has been interested in Fort Jesup since he was a young child visiting the site on school trips and family visits. He began volunteering at the site while in high school in 1995 and the next year was hired to be a tour guide and researcher. He continued to work at the site through college and served as a lab assistant for the Fort Jesup Archeological Field School. DeBose received a bachelor of arts in history and a bachelor of arts in anthropology in 2003 and a master of music in 2010 from Northwestern State University. DeBose is currently the director of bands at Many High School and president of the Friends of Fort Jesup, Inc. He lives in Many, Louisiana, with his wife and four children.